Essential Java *Fast*

How to write object oriented software for the Internet

Springer

London
Berlin
Heidelberg
New York
Barcelona
Budapest
Hong Kong
Milan
Paris
Santa Clara
Singapore
Tokyo

John Cowell

Essential
Java *Fast*

How to write object oriented
software for the Internet

with 64 figures

Springer

John Cowell, BSc(Hons), MPhil.,PhD.
Department of Computer and Information Sciences, De Montfort University
Kents Hill Campus, Hammerwood Gate, Kents Hill
Milton Keynes. MK7 6HP, UK

ISBN 3-540-76052-0 Springer-Verlag Berlin Heidelberg New York

British Library Cataloguing in Publication Data
Cowell, John, 1957–
    Essential Java fast : how to write object oriented software for the Internet in Java
    1.Java (Computer program language) 2.Object-oriented programming (Computer science)
    3.Internet (Computer network)
    I.Title
    005.1 ' 33
    ISBN 3540760520

Library of Congress Cataloging-in-Publication Data
A Catalog record for this book is available from the Library of Congress

© Springer-Verlag London Limited 1997
Printed in Great Britain

Typesetting : camera-ready by author
Printed and bound by Athenæum Press, Gateshead, England
34/3830-543210. Printed on acid-free paper

Contents

1

Why Use Java?

Introduction

In early 1997 there were over 50 million Internet users, with new subscriptions growing by over a 100 per cent every year. It is estimated that by 2002 there will be over 200 million Internet users.

One of the most important parts of the Internet is the World Wide Web. There are over 100,000 Web sites - 75% in the US and about 10% in the UK. Since its introduction in the early 90's the Web has been one of the greatest success stories in the computer business. It provides a way of exchanging information globally at very low cost. For the price of a PC and a local phone call, you can read text and graphics which are stored anywhere in the world.

It is easy to navigate the Web either for serious work or just for fun using a browser program such as Netscape, Hot Java, or the Internet Explorer. The information on the Web is organised in pages which have a unique name, just give the name to your browser and it will find the page for you wherever it is in the world. The only disappointing thing about the Web (apart from its speed!) is that it is only possible to interact with Web pages in a limited way. Web pages are written in a language called .HTML, you can read them, jump to other related pages and download information, but nothing more. This is not too surprising when you consider that you could be browsing using a PC, a UNIX workstation, a VAX, or any other type of computer. It is a major achievement that you can even use the World Wide Web with this range of computers. Java extends the capabilities of the Web and overcomes these limitations. A Java program can be embedded in an HTML Web page, so that you can add moving graphics and create fully interactive pages.

Why should you use Java? It is being taken up by virtually all the major software companies and is certain to be an integral part of interactive Web applications for many years to come. It has become the industry standard in the past twelve months More importantly perhaps, it is currently the only way of writing these applications.

What is Java?

Java is the latest programming language from Sun Microsystems. It allows you to write two types of programs:

- Applets, which can only run within your net browser.
- Applications, which run as stand alone programs on your computer, without using a browser.

If you want to write stand alone programs, you have a wide range of languages to choose from, of which Java is one. If you want to write interactive Web pages, Java is the only serious language that you can use, and has already become the world standard. A major bonus is that you can write your applets in Java whatever type of computer you are using, including mainframes, VAXs, workstations and PCs.

Is this book for you?

This book assumes that you have used a high level programming language such as Pascal. A knowledge of C or especially C++ will be an even greater help, but this is not essential. This book provides a complete introduction to Java and its development environment. It will give you enough information to develop serious, professional interactive applications for the World Wide Web.

The browser used to test all the applets was Netscape V2.02, however since Java is platform independent (that is will run on any host computer) all of the applets will work equally within any browser that supports Java.

It is assumed that you have some experience of using Windows 95 programs such as word processors, spreadsheets or databases, and know how to use a Web browser such as Netscape or Hot Java.

It is helpful if you already have some programming experience, but all the essential elements of Java are covered. If you have used C or C++ you will be able to switch to Java even faster.

The support information for Java is available from the Sun Microsystems Web site and while this is helpful and well written, it is not complete and does not present the information in a clear and well organised format. It can be very frustrating if you are trying to find out about a particular feature of Java to complete your application, when access is slow and you cannot find the right page quickly. This is becoming an increasing problem as the number of users on the Web increases and greater demands are placed on the infra-structure of the Internet.

This book aims to give you a grasp of all the most important features of the language. There are many illustrations and examples. The best way to learn Java is to try out the examples for yourself.

What you need to run Java

The computer used to develop all the applications and applets in this book was a Pentium PC with 16MB of memory. This gave excellent performance, but you can develop and run applets successfully on a less powerful computer. Java is not a large application by modern standards, so disk capacity is unlikely to be a problem. In common with most Windows 95 programs, Java programs can be developed with a modest configuration but they will not run fast. The minimum computer that you need so that the performance is adequate is:

- Intel 80486DX2 or better.
- 8MB or more of memory.
- 50 MB of disk space for a full installation

The most important factor in limiting performance is likely to be memory. Netscape and Java run much faster with 16Mb of memory. A Pentium processor is ideal.

This book uses Sun's Java development environment - which you can download from the Sun Web site - the address is http://java.sun.com/.

How to use this book

If you want to develop applets in Java, a free toolkit is available on the Sun Microsystems Web site. Cynics may say that the fact it is free accounts for its great popularity, but this is unfair, Java is a powerful object oriented language that is ideal for writing interactive Web applications.

Designing and writing software is a complex job and a wide range of methods have been developed to help us write software with fewer bugs. The methodology which is being increasingly adopted is object orientation. A lot of people are put off object orientation by the jargon which surrounds it, but when you get beyond that (this book will help you to do that), you will see that it has significant benefits over any other technique. Object orientation is a powerful way of modelling real-world problems and it has deservedly become the preferred way of designing applications. It is worthwhile gaining an understanding of the key concepts of object orientation before starting to use Java, as it will make it easier for you to develop successful applications.

To appreciate just how good an object oriented language Java is, you need to know the concepts behind object oriented programming. This book describes the essential principles of object oriented design and after even after the first few chapters you will be able to develop substantial applications. The later chapters look at more complex aspects of Java.

You do not need to read all of the chapters of this book before you can use Java, in fact, the best way to learn Java is to try the example programs on your own computer. If you do want to develop more complex applications or you are interested in a particular aspect of Java, you can go directly to the relevant chapters after you have read the earlier introductory material.

This book is not intended to be a definitive description of Java - if it did it would be about ten times as long and take twenty times as long to read. The philosophy of this book is to cover the key features of Java so that you can write applications as soon as possible.

Becoming fluent in a new programming language is difficult and time consuming. Fortunately you do not have to be fluent to produce useful applications. It is best not to try and learn every aspect of the language before you write your first Java applet. The best way to learn Java is to read the early chapters and to try the examples for yourself.

There is a lot of hype around the Java language which for once is not exaggerated. Java is an excellent new language which will allow you to develop interactive applications for the Web *fast* - you do not even need to read all of this book before you can start!

Conventions

There are a few conventions used in this book which make it easier to read:

- All program examples are in *italics*.
- File names and identifiers are in *italics*.
- Class names always start with a capital.
- Variables and packages never start with a capital.
- When a name is composed of more than one word, the start letter of each word is a capital, for example, the variable name *myLongIdentifierName*.

The conventions for naming variables, classes, files and so on are not mandatory, but they have been adopted world wide by Java users.

2
Object Orientation Primer

Introduction

Designing large applications is a complicated process and fraught with difficulties. While hardware always behaves in a predictable way the same is not true of software. All the applications we use have some sort of bugs in them. Even if an application was perfect it would be virtually impossible to prove it. In recent years there have been a number of design methodologies which provide a way of designing software to minimise the errors. The latest in this long list is object oriented design and programming. Since object oriented programming is widely regarded as the best way of writing software with the least bugs, many companies have claimed that their product is object oriented, while lacking many of the key features of object orientation, which we look at in this chapter.

Java is a truly object oriented programming language, but if you are not used to working with this sort of language it can seem strange at first, and it is tempting to try and miss out on this key feature of the language and write your applications or applets as if you were writing them in C. This will cause problems later though, and it is worthwhile spending the time reading this chapter to get a grasp of the main aspects of object oriented programming. There is a lot of jargon used in object orientation but all the key terms that you need to know to develop effective applets in Java are covered in this chapter.

In this chapter you will learn:

- What objects are.
- The difference between objects and classes.
- What attributes are.
- The importance of inheritance.

What are objects?

We view the external world in terms of objects, such as your computer, your bike, buildings, animals and plants. In an application we have objects such as buttons, and list boxes.

Most objects are made up out of other objects, your bike has, for example, a frame, wheels, pedals and so on. If we know that we can build a bike by combining these objects then we do not need to worry about the design and structure of each of these objects - which may be very complex. Each wheel will have spokes, bearings and tyres, but we do not need to know the detail of how the wheel works, we just need to know that we attach one at each end of the bike frame. The advantage of this is that we can combine each of these objects without any detailed knowledge of what is going on inside them. These days if the disk drive on your computer stops working, you simply replace the drive, without looking at its internal components and trying to fix it, that is the drive is viewed as an object. If it is connected in a particular way to the motherboard of your computer, it will carry out a defined action (reading and writing data). Similarly in object oriented programming if we have objects which behave in a defined way, we can combine them together to make an application without worrying about what happens inside each object. If I have a software object which sorts numbers in order of size all I have to do is present the numbers to that object and wait until it returns the sorted values to me. I do not have to worry about how it actually carries out the sorting. The key to object oriented programming is to view your application as a number of objects which interact with each other. You can concentrate on the internal design of an object without having to worry about the effect it will have on other objects, providing the interface between objects is clearly defined.

Classes

One of the most common areas of confusion in object oriented programming is between objects and classes. In the real world there are many objects which are of the same type. This is a useful way of grouping objects which share some characteristics. All books in the world are members of a *book* class, which has certain characteristics or attributes. All books have pages, a cover, and contain words or pictures. This book is a *book* object, that is a member of the class of *book*. In object oriented jargon, this book is an instance of the class *book*.

An object oriented language allows you to create classes and objects which belong to these classes. Before we move on to look at how this works in practice, let us look at another example, since the ideas of classes, instances and objects are crucial to working in Java.

Another class is the *Building* class. There are many buildings, but at this moment if you are indoors, you are in just one of those. *Building* is the class, that is the template for all buildings, but the building you are in, is an instance of that class. Each instance is an object.

The class does not refer to any building in particular, it is just the template that describes all buildings. An instance of the *Building* class is a particular building, that is, it is an object. An instance of any class is an object. Clearly all of these buildings shown in fig 2.1 are very different, but they all share a common set of attributes, for example they all have floors, and walls and are used as places for people to live, work or play in.

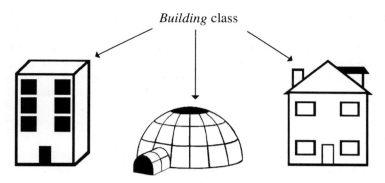

Fig. 2.1 *Three instances of the Building class.*

Attributes and behaviour

All instances of a class (that is all objects of that class) share the same attributes, for example, a few of the attributes for the *Building* class may be:

- The number of floors.
- The number of windows.
- The floor area.
- The use of the building, for example work, recreation, or storage.

However, the values of these attributes are different for different buildings and are therefore called instance variables. The instance variables may remain constant for the life of the object (such as the number of floors of the building), or may change (such as the use of the building).

In addition to objects having instance variables, every class defines a set of operations which may be performed on each of these objects to change the value of the instance variables or to provide information about the state of these variables. If the function of building is to be changed from work to recreation then there must be an operation that will allow this to happen. Similarly there must be a set of operations that will report on the state of the variables.

In terms of software, the class provides a blueprint or template that defines both the variables and the operations that can be performed. These operations are called methods.

After a class has been defined, objects belonging to that class, that is instances, can be created. Java provides many classes for you to use, so there you do not have to start from scratch every time you want to write an application.

Inheritance

Classes define a template for objects, but sometimes it is helpful to divide a class into a number of subclasses each of which share some characteristics but not all, for example the *Building* class could be divided into the subclasses of *House*, *OfficeBlock* and *Garage* as shown in fig 2.2.

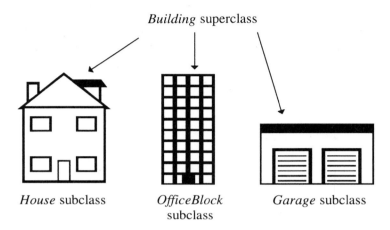

House subclass   *OfficeBlock*   *Garage* subclass
                          subclass

Fig. 2.2 *Class hierarchy for the Building superclass.*

Building is the superclass of the subclasses *House*, *OfficeBlock* and *Garage* (and of the many other types of buildings not mentioned).

Every subclass inherits the attributes of the superclass and all the methods that operate on the superclass, for example, *House, OfficeBlock*, and *Garage* all share the attribute which defines the use of the building, and the methods which are used to display or change this attribute, for example, to display its current use.

Subclasses can do more however, than simply inheriting all the attributes and methods of the superclass. Subclasses can have additional variables and methods to those of the superclass, for example the *Garage* subclass could have an attribute which specifies the number of cars which can be parked in it and some associated methods. Subclasses can also override methods which are inherited from the superclass, for example you may wish to change the method which amends the number of floors of the *Garage* subclass so that it does not allow more than one floor.

You can have many layers of inheritance in your inheritance tree or class hierarchy.

Why use inheritance?

If you can reuse your existing code or use existing class libraries you can be more productive, and if the classes you are using have been fully tested you can write code with fewer bugs in it. One of the key features of object oriented programming is that it allows you to reuse code, subclasses inherit the attributes and methods of the superclass and you only need to add those methods and variables that provide the specialised behaviour required by your application.

Java makes extensive use of abstract classes, that is superclasses which provide generic behaviour, in fact all classes in Java are subclasses of one superclass. An abstract class leaves much of the class definition not implemented so that the subclasses can define specialised behaviour.

The Java toolkit provides several collections of Java classes in packages. Packages are groups of classes which perform similar operations. The Abstract Windowing Toolkit (AWT) is one such package which provides a set of classes which can be used for displaying and controlling windows, buttons, list boxes, menus and so on.

3
Java Applets

Introduction

Java is an excellent language for writing applications. It is object orientated, it has a similar syntax to the popular C++ language and an extensive set of supporting classes available. If you are developing a stand alone application, Java is a good choice, but if you want to write an application that can be run across the Internet on any platform, from a PC to a mainframe, Java is the only choice. Any computer which has a browser such as Netscape or HotJava can run Java applications, or applets as they are called.

Because Java applets are downloaded to the host computer and executed automatically there are some limitations on what applets can do. For example, accessing the local file system of the host computer is restricted, as the organisation of files and directories will be different for every computer that the applet runs on. Another problem with allowing a foreign application access to your hard disk is that your computer could contract a virus. This is one of the more controversial aspects of Java that has not yet been resolved. If your computer has ever contracted a virus, you know that it is not a problem to be ignored. One way of minimising the risks is to regularly run one of the many virus checking programs, particularly if you often download software from the Internet.

In this chapter you will learn:

- The differences between applications and applets.
- Why Java is different from other languages.
- How to incorporate Java applets into HTML pages.
- How to create, start and stop applets.
- How to pass parameters to applets and applications.

Applets and applications

Applets differ from applications in that they run within HTML pages when viewed by Web browsers which support Java such as Netscape and HotJava. This ability allows designers much greater flexibility in the material they can include on Web pages. Applets can be run on any computer.

Applications run only on the specific computer or family of computers they are compiled for. They do not run within the browser.

The Java language is very similar for both applications and applets, however there are some differences between applets and applications caused by the environments in which they run:

- Applets may not be able to read or write to files on the host computer. This is because applets can run on any platform which supports a browser with a Java interpreter and files systems are different on different computers. There are also serious security implications of doing this.
- Applets cannot load or run local programs or refer to DLLs.
- Applets cannot communicate with the local server.

However despite these understandable limitations there are some benefits to working within the browser environment in particular:

- A good user interface.
- Access to event handling.
- Access to a networking environment.
- Improved graphics capabilities.

In addition, there are a few differences between the structure of applets and applications that we look at later. Most of the examples in this book are applets, since this is the main way in which Java is used, however in some cases it is easier to illustrate points without the added complexities of using a browser and an HTML file. In these circumstances applications are used.

Why applets are different

In a conventional programming language, an application is written as a series of source files in a language such as Pascal or C. The file extension indicates what the programming language is, for example PAS for Pascal and CPP for C++. These files are compiled to produce relocatable binary object modules or object files, which have an extension of OBJ, as shown in fig 3.1.

The object files and any library files are combined together with a linker to give an executable file with an EXE extension.

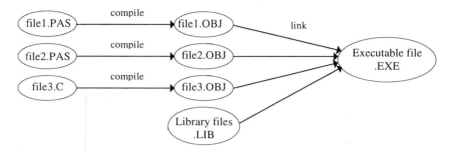

Fig. 3.1 *Creating an application in a conventional environment.*

The application program can only be run on the system for which it was compiled and linked, so you need different compilers and linkers for different types of computer. This was fine when people worked on their own computer or even on a network of the same type of computers, but caused real problems when computers were linked together on the Internet. How can a PC, a Sun workstation, a DEC VAX and an IBM mainframe share information without worrying about the radically different architectures and organisation of these computers?

HTML, (Hyper Text Mark-up Language) provides a standard format that can be understood by browsers such as Netscape and Hot Java. If you use the World Wide Web, the pages that you see are written in HTML, and we take it for granted that you can view these pages on any type of computer, but it is remarkable that one standard has been accepted and that we can do this. It would be chaos if the pages you could view were dependent on the computer you were using.

HTML is a standard, however it is changing quite rapidly at the moment, as new features are added, although the changes are usually "backward compatible", that is old HTML pages will still work in a new HTML environment.

HTML is quite limited in what it can do, and you cannot develop interactive applications with it. To get around this problem, Java was developed which allows programs to be run on any computer within the browser. A Java application which is run within a browser is called an applet. To create an applet:

- Write your Java source code, which must be in a file with a java extension.
- Compile the source code into a file with a class extension.
- Write an HTML file with an APPLET tag which refers to the name of your class file.
- Run the browser and ask it to execute the HTML file. When it reads the HTML file it will find the APPLET tag and so execute your Java applet.

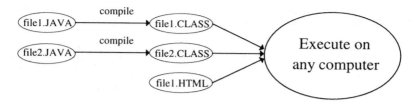

Fig. 3.2 *Creating an application in a conventional environment.*

The HTML and class files will run on any computer which supports Java, this can either be a local computer or one across the Internet, which can access the HTML file in exactly the same way as it would access any other HTML page.

At the moment, Java is the only way of creating interactive applications, but I do not intend to argue that you should use Java because it is all that is available! Java is based on the highly successful C++ language. Many programmers who want to write software for the Internet already know C++ and so this makes learning Java a lot easier.

Java, like C++, is an object oriented language, which is considered by most experts to be the best way of creating applications with the minimum of bugs. Object oriented languages allow you to create reusable objects that will speed up your application development and save you having to write the same code more than once.

A Simple applet

In this section we are going to look at the structure of a Java applet. All the ideas introduced here are used throughout the book, so you will have a chance to use them.

There are five key methods in Java applications. If you do not include your own version of these methods, Java will use a default method for each. The methods are:

- *init.*
- *start.*
- *stop.*
- *destroy.*
- *paint.*

Initialising an applet

When a Java applet runs, the first method which is executed is the *init* method. There is no *main* method in an applet. This method can be used to initialise values, or for loading images which are used later. Java provides its own *init* method, but you can include your own and override the default. The *init* method looks like this:

```
public void init( ) {
...
}
```

Starting an applet

The *start* method is called next. Unlike *init* this may be called many times in the life of your program, whenever you switch to another page, the applet stops running, when you return to the page, the *start* method is executed again. The *start* method looks like this:

```
public void start( ) {
    ...
}
```

Stopping an applet

The *stop* method is the partner of the *start* method and stops an applet running. Whenever you leave a page the applet continues running, however you can override this and stop execution until you return to the page:

```
public void stop( ) {
    ...
}
```

Destroying an applet

Destroying an applet ensures that any threads the applet has created and any system resources that it has used are released. Usually this is done for you by the default *destroy* method and you will not need to override it:

```
public void destroy( ) {
    ...
}
```

Displaying text and graphics

Whenever the applet displays text or a graphic on the page, the *paint* method is used. It is also called when the screen is redrawn, if, for example, another window is obscuring the Web page and this window is closed to display the Web page.

```
public void paint (Graphics g){
    ...
}
```

The *paint* method is called many times in the life of a typical applet, so it is important to keep the minimum amount of code in it, so that it executes as fast as possible.

The *paint* method takes an argument, an instance of the *Graphics* class. This object is created automatically for you, but you do need to make sure that the *Graphics* class is imported into your applet by using an *import* statement at the top of the applet:

> *import java.awt.Graphics*

If you are including other classes such as *Color* you can explicitly include this with an *import* statement or you can use a wild card in your *import* statement:

> *import.java.awt.**

Java applets are easily incorporated into HTML pages with the minimum of effort - so you do not lose all the benefits of using HTML.

Java and HTML

Web pages are written in HTML. A simple HTML file is shown below, which does not run a Java applet. Each of the items between the < > brackets is called a tag.

> *<HTML>*
> *<!This is the hello program>*
> *<HEAD>*
> *<TITLE> The Hello program </TITLE>*
> *</HEAD>*
> *<BODY>*
> *Hello everyone*
> *</BODY>*
> *</HTML>*

If you run your browser and open this HTML file you will see a screen which is similar to the one shown in fig. 3.3.

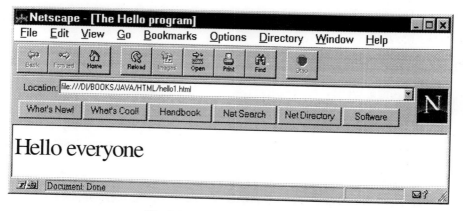

Fig 3.3. The Hello program.

HTML tags

Each of the HTML tags is interpreted by the browser.

- The <HTML> tag indicates the start of an HTML document.
- The </HTML> tag indicates the end of the HTML document.
- The <!.....> tag contains a comment which is not displayed by the browser.
- The <HEAD> and </HEAD> are the start and end of the document meta information and contain information about the document, such as its title.
- The text following the <TITLE> tag is the heading which appears on the bar at the top of the browser.
- The </TITLE> tag indicates the end of the title text.
- The <BODY> and </BODY> tags indicate the start and end of the document which is displayed by the browser.

The applet tag

Applets are included in Web pages by the use of the <APPLET> tag. When a Java-aware Web browser downloads a page that includes a reference to a Java applet, the applet is also downloaded and then executed. The <APPLET> tag has various options that control the size and position of the applet's space on the Web page, the alignment with surrounding text and graphics, and parameters that can be supplied to the applet.

The <APPLET> tag is included within the body of the HTML file, that is between the <BODY> and </BODY> tags which specify the start and end of the body:

```
<BODY>
<APPLET CODE = "Hello.class" WIDTH=150 HEIGHT=25>
</APPLET>
</BODY>
```

The source code for the applet is in a file called *Hello.java*. When this is compiled the class file *Hello.class* is created.

The WIDTH and HEIGHT tags define the area of the page within which the applet runs.

If you define more than one class in a Java source file, a file with a class extension is produced for each class you have defined as shown in fig 3.4.

This can sometimes cause confusion if you are expecting only one class file to be produced.

The name of the HTML file in this example must be the same as the name of the class files which starts the applet. In this case there are three files:

- *Hello.java*, this is the source file.
- *Hello.class* is the class file produced when *Hello.java* is compiled.
- *Hello.html.* is the HTML file which has the <APPLET> tag in it.

If you have more than one class in your applet, the name of the HTML file must still be the same as the name of the class which starts the applet.

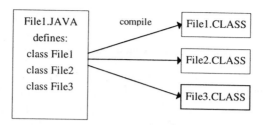

Fig. 3.4 *Compiling Java files to produce class files.*

Creating an applet

Do not be too concerned if you are feeling swamped by theory at this stage. The best way to learn a language is to use it to write your own programs. In this section we are going to create an applet and then show how it is combined with a number of HTML tags which control the position of the applet and the HTML text on the page.

The applet displays the text *Java applet*. Most computers support a wide range of fonts, such as Times Roman, Courier, and Arial. The size of these fonts is measured in points. There are usually **bold** and *italic* versions of these fonts. The text displayed by this applet is in 30 point Italic Times Roman.

The full listing of the applet source file *Hello.java* is given below:

```
import java.awt.*;
public class Hello extends java.applet.Applet {
    public void paint (graphics g){
        Font myFont = new Font("TimesRoman", Font.ITALIC, 30);
        g.setFont(myFont);
        g.drawString("Java applet", 5, 20);
    }
}
```

The first line imports the *Graphics* class into your applet. You can have as many *import* statements as required. The *Graphics* class is supplied with Java in a package which is a group of related classes.

Next the *Hello* class is defined as being *public,* which means that this class is visible to any other class. The next part of the line *extends java.applet.Applet* states that the *Hello* class is a subclass of the *Applet* class.

Although the first two lines of this applet look complicated, every applet that you produce will start in virtually the same way.

The default *paint* method is overridden in this applet since a custom *paint* method is included.

The *paint* method creates a new italic Times Roman font of size thirty. The *setFont* method assigns this font to be the default font, so that all text which is subsequently drawn is of this type. Finally it displays the text *Java Applet* at position 5,20 using the *drawString* method.

The default *init, start, stop* and *destroy* methods are implicitly used and do not have to be defined.

When you have created your source file which must have an extension of *java*, you need to compile it. You can compile the file *Hello.java* by running the Java compiler:

        javac Hello.java

This will produce the file *Hello.class*, which is the file you refer to in your HTML APPLET tag. There must be a class called *Hello* defined in the file *Hello.java*.

Applets need to run from an HTML file by using an <APPLET> tag within the body of the HTML file. The complete HTML file is shown below:

```
<HTML>
<!This applet displays a message>
<HEAD>
<TITLE> The Hello program </TITLE>
</HEAD>
<BODY>
<APPLET CODE> = "Hello.class" WIDTH = 150 HEIGHT = 25>
</APPLET>
 </BODY>
</HTML>
```

This file must be called *Hello.html*. To run this applet open this HTML page from your browser.

Controlling the applet size and position

Your pages will usually be a mixture of text and graphics supplied by HTML and your Java applet. There are some HTML commands that control the position of your applet.

It is worthwhile trying these examples, to do this, you need to amend the HTML file from the previous example:

```
<HTML>
<!This applet displays a message>
<HEAD>
<TITLE> The Hello program</TITLE>
</HEAD>
<BODY>
<APPLET CODE> = "Hello.class" WIDTH = 150 HEIGHT = 25>
</APPLET>
 </BODY>
</HTML>
```

When you change your HTML file you do not need to compile your applet every time.

There are some bugs in Netscape V2.02 and earlier which in some circumstances may cause problems when trying some of these examples, particularly when using the

ALIGN attribute. There is a particularly annoying bug that occurs if you follow this sequence of actions

- Run Netscape.
- Run your applet within Netscape.
- Exit Netscape without shutting it down.
- Change and recompile the Java source file.
- Return to Netscape.
- Run your applet again

You will find that Netscape still picks up the old applet from memory, although it should be possible to prevent this, there seems to be no way around it. The only solution is to close Netscape and run it again.

This can cause a lot of frustrating time wasting if you are not aware of what is happening.

There are also occasionally problems with Netscape when using the ALIGN property, which causes the applet not to start running.

Hopefully both of these problems will be fixed in later releases.

The size of the applet is determined by the HEIGHT and WIDTH attributes, for example:

<APPLET CODE = "Hello.class" WIDTH = 200 HEIGHT = 25>

The position of the applet is determined by the ALIGN property. This can have 9 values, but the most commonly used are LEFT and RIGHT.

When the ALIGN attribute is assigned to LEFT or RIGHT the HTML text flows around the applet as shown in fig 3.5.

<APPLET CODE = "Hello.class" WIDTH = 200 HEIGHT = 25
ALIGN=RIGHT>
<\APPLET>
This text will wrap around the Java applet which is placed on the far right of the page since the ALIGN attribute = RIGHT

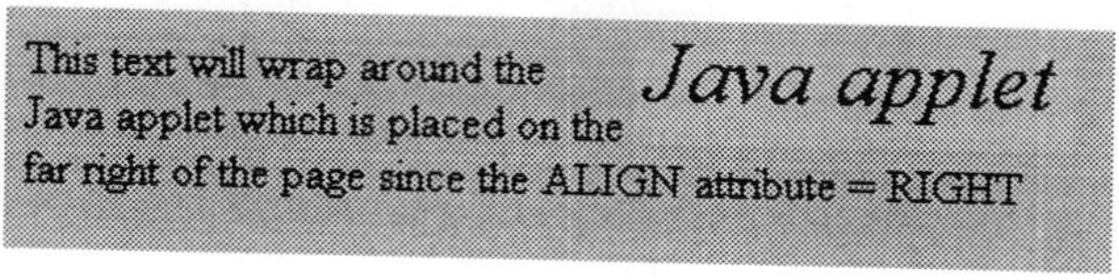

Fig. 3.5 *The ALIGN attribute = RIGHT.*

In addition to LEFT and RIGHT there are seven other values for the ALIGN attribute. These seven are only used if the applet is to be placed within a single line of text. These are listed in Table 3.1

Table 3.1 *Values of the ALIGN attribute.*

Value	Effect
MIDDLE	The middle of the applet is aligned with the middle of the line of text.
ABSMIDDLE	The middle of the applet is aligned with the middle of the largest element of the line.
TOP	Aligns the top of the applet with the top of the line.
TEXTTOP	Aligns the top of the applet with the top of the highest element in the line
BOTTOM	Aligns the bottom of the applet with the bottom of the text.
ABSBOTTOM	Aligns the bottom of the applet with the lowest element in the line.
BASELINE	The same as BOTTOM

One of the most commonly used values is TOP, for example:

> *<APPLET CODE = "Hello.class" WIDTH = 200 HEIGHT = 25*
> *ALIGN=TOP>*
> *<\APPLET>*
> *This text will wrap around the Java applet with the top of the applet aligned with the top of the text. The text does not wrap around the applet. The ALIGN attribute = TOP*

The effect of a similar HTML file and applet is shown in fig 3.6 with the ALIGN parameter changed to TOP.

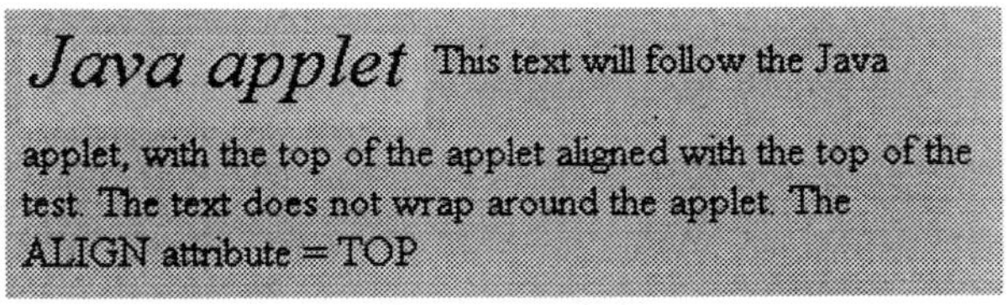

Fig. 3.6 *The ALIGN attribute = TOP.*

The applet is placed in a single line of text with the top of the applet aligned with the top of the line of text. Subsequent text does not wrap around the applet but is placed below it.

If you are using Netscape version 2.02 or earlier there are some bugs which may mean that the ALIGN attribute does not always work correctly.

You can control the amount of space around the applet by using the HSPACE and VSPACE attributes.

Compiling applications

If you have written a stand alone application rather than an applet, you compile it in the same way, but to run it you need to use the Java interpreter. A source file called *MyApplication.java* is compiled by typing:

> *javac MyApplication.java*

and run by typing:

> *Java MyApplication*

If you have written an application rather than an applet, you do not need a browser or an HTML file to run it.

Command line arguments for applications

Some applications need to have information passed to them at run-time. These are called command line arguments. For example if you have a sort application you may have to specify the name of the file to be sorted and the name of the output file containing the sorted information.

In Java programs there is only one parameter passed to the application:

- *args*: an array of strings containing the arguments.

The number of arguments can be found from using the *length( )* method of the array.

To run a Java application called *sort* and to pass two parameters *infile* and *outfile* the following command line is needed:

> *javac sort infile outfile*

The first argument is *infile*.

If you are familiar with C++, you will notice that this language uses a similar mechanism to Java. The differences between C++ and Java in this and many other areas are described in chapter 15.

Command line arguments for applets

While you can pass command line arguments to a Java application using the *main* method, you cannot do this with applets, since they do not have a *main* method or a command line, so how are parameters passed to them? You need to add a new attribute to your HTML file, for example:

> *<APPLET CODE = "Hello.class">*
> *<PARAM NAME = theName VALUE = "John">*
> *</APPLET>*

You also need to change the *init* method in your Java code to receive this parameter using the *getParameter* method. You must specify the same name as in the HTML file, that is *theName*. The names of the parameters are case sensitive.

The corresponding Java code is:

```
import java.awt.Graphics;
public class Hello extends java.applet.Applet {
    String myName;
    public void init( ) {
        String myName = getParameter("theName");
    }

    public void paint (graphics g){
        g.drawString("Hello "+ , myName, 5, 20);
    }
}
```

This will print out the message *Hello John*.

If you used the *getParameter* method to pick up a value from the HTML file and one was not supplied, a null value would be assigned to the string value.

The parameters passed from the HTML are always strings, so if you want to pass, for example, an integer value you get the parameter in the same way using the *getParameter* method and then convert it to an integer using the *Integer.parseInt* method.

If you wanted to print the hello message more than once, you would specify this using a second parameter called *theNumber*. The HTML would look like this:

```
<APPLET CODE = "Hello.class">
<PARAM NAME = theName VALUE= "John">
<PARAM NAME = theNumber VALUE = "3">
</APPLET>
```

The Java code looks like this:

```
import java.awt.Graphics;
public class Hello extends java.applet.Applet {
    String myName, n;
    int number;
public void init( ) {
    String myName = getParameter("theName");
    String n = getParameter("theNumber);
    number = Integer.parseInt(n);
}

public void paint (graphics g){
    for (c=0; c<number; c++) {
        g.drawString("Hello "+ , myName, 5, 20 + c*20);
    }
```

```
                }
        }
```

The statement:

number = Integer.parseInt(n);

converts the string "3" into the numerical value 3.

The applet prints out the message *Hello John* on three successive lines.

- VSPACE determines the space both above and below the applet. These are the same value.
- HSPACE determines the space to the right and left of the applet, again these are the same.

4

The Java Language

Introduction

The Java programming language is similar to the C++ language - but with some interesting differences. If you are a C++ expert you will be able to zip through this chapter quite fast - chapter 15 deals specifically with the differences between the two languages. If you have used a high level language such as Pascal before you will also find the switch to Java straightforward.

In this chapter you will learn about :

- The organisation of Java programs
- Java statements.
- Using variables.
- Operators.

Applications and applets

Java can be used for writing programs which run directly on computers via the Java interpreter without using a Web browser. Programs which run like this are called *applications*.

The major use of Java however, is to write programs which can be run within the environment provided by a Web browser such as Netscape or HotJava. These types of programs are called *applets*.

This chapter is concerned with the Java language without introducing the added complexity of creating applets which work within the browser environments and so the examples are mainly applications, which are not run within the browser.

Features of Java programs

Before we look at how to write Java programs it is worthwhile looking at some of the conventions that Java uses.

One feature of Java that is often more of a hindrance than a help is that Java is case sensitive. *MyJavaApplet* is different from *MyJavaapplet*. The convention in Java is that class names are capitalised, for example:

class FloatToInt

Everything else including methods and objects (we look at these later) is in lower case, for example:

int count;
float value;

If you choose a name which is made up of more than one word, the first letter of the second and subsequent words are capitalised, for example:

int myInt;
float myLargeFloat;

Java allows a fairly free layout, white space such as spaces and tabs are ignored by the compiler, as are comments. In common with C++ there are two ways of specifying comments:

/* This is a comment which goes over more than
one line, delimited by the slash and star as shown */

// This is a single line of comment indicated by two slashes.

Java statements are terminated by a semicolon at the end of the statement. This is a common source of error for new Java programmers.

Names in Java

In Java you will need to name variables, classes and methods. There are a few rules that define what names you can use:

- A name must start with a letter, an underscore (_) or a dollar sign($).
- Subsequent characters can be any printable character except for a few reserved characters listed in Appendix A

Running a Java application

In order to run the Java application you need to compile it. You do this by returning to the command line prompt and typing:

javac MyProgram.java

The code is in a file called *MyProgram.java*. The output from the compiler will be one file with a *class* extension for every class in the file. In this case *MyProgram.class* alone is produced.

To run the program type:

> *java MyProgram*

This invokes the Java interpreter which will execute your program.

Key elements of a Java program

All Java applications and applets will contain the following elements:

- Class definitions.
- Objects. These are instances of a defined class.
- Data variables.
- Methods, which define the operations that can be performed on the data.

In this chapter we are going to look at each of these elements.

Classes

Everything in Java is in a class, or describes what a class does. Java, unlike most other programming languages, does not have functions or procedures, instead programs are broken up into class blocks,

If you were programming in C these classes would be replaced by functions.

As you would expect, classes start with the reserved word *class*. This is followed by the name of the class and an open brace.

The definition of a simple class is shown below:

> *class NewClass {*
>   ...
> *}*

If this class is a subclass of another class you need to use the *extends* directive to indicate this, for example:

> *class AnotherNewClass extends NewClass {*
>   ...
> *}*

The set of operations that can operate on a class are called the methods. These are defined within the class.

New objects

A class is a form of template which describes the characteristics of a set of objects. After you have created a class you are able to define objects which are instances of classes. To create an object you need to provide the following:

- The name of the class that you want to create an instance of.
- The name of the object you are creating.
- The keyword *new*.
- The name of the class again, followed by brackets. When creating some new objects you need to specify some initial values between these brackets.

Two examples are shown below:

> *Building myHouse = new Building( );*
> *Random value = new Random( );*

The first line creates a new object called *myHouse*, the second a new object called *value*.

An equivalent way of creating the *value* objects is:

> *Random value;*
> *value = new Random( );*

The *new* keyword actually creates the new instance of the object. It allocates the memory required by the object. It initialises any variables, for example it assigns booleans to false and it calls the constructor method for the object. Constructors are covered later in this chapter.

Data types

In Java before you can use a variable you have to define it by giving it a type. If you want you can also give the variable a value at the same time. Local variables are defined within methods.

Java does not have any global variables that are available to all methods of the application, however you can define instance variables and class variables which you will look at later in this chapter, which allow variables to be shared within classes.

To declare a variable specify the type followed by the variable, for example:

> *int first, second, third;*   *// creates three integer variables*
> *int oldAge, newAge=50;*   *// newAge=50, oldAge is unassigned*
> *boolean onOff;*   *// creates a boolean variable*

The table 4.1 gives a full list of the primitive Java data types and the number of bits allocated to each type.

One surprising feature of the list of types, is that characters take up 16 bits rather than 8. In Java characters are stored as the Unicode character number. Note also that boolean values are allocated 8 bits.

One noticeable omission if you have done some Java programming before is that *String* is not included in the list of primitive Java data types. This is because a string is not a primitive data type, but an instance of the *String* class, that is an object. The clue to this is that the keyword *String* always starts with a capital letter, indicating that it is a class. You can however create and use *String* objects as if they were variables of one of the primitive data types.

Table 4.1 *The primitive Java data types.*

Type	Description	Number of bits
byte	integer	8
short	integer	16
int	integer	32
long	integer	64
float	floating point	32
double	floating point	64
char	character	16
logical	boolean	8

Arrays

Arrays are lists of items. Each item in the list is of the same type, which is one of the primitive Java types. In Java, arrays are used differently to most third generation programming languages such as C and Pascal. Particularly if you are an experienced programmer the way in which Java treats arrays can cause problems. In Java arrays are objects.

To declare an array you specify the type of the array followed by its name, for example:

> *int values[ ];*
> *String myStringArray[ ];*

An alternative notation is:

> *int[ ] values;*
> *String[ ] myStringArray;*

Just pick one of these and stick with it for consistency.

Next you have to create an array object. There are two ways of doing this. You can use *new*:

> *int[ ] values = new int[5];*

This creates a list of 5 integer items. The first is referred to as *values[0]* and the last as *value[4]*.

The array elements are initialised, 0 for numbers, false for booleans, null for strings and \0 for characters.

An alternative is to specify the initial values of the array elements:

> *int[ ] values = {3, 45, 87, 23,9};*

This defines a five element array of integers and assigns *value[0]* the number 3, *value[1]* the number 45 and so on.

When strings are initialised each string item is enclosed in quotes:

String[ ] languages = {"Java", "C++", "Object Pascal"};

If you want to change an array element you do so by specifying its name and the element that you want to change:

languages[2] = "Visual Basic";

A common problem in C++ is that if you define an array as having, for example, 10 elements and you try and write to an element greater than this at run time, unexpected problems can happen. It may cause the program to halt and give an error message or the program may continue having overwritten a piece of data that happened to be at the place in the memory than you wrote to. This can cause chaos. Java has resolved this problem and checks to ensure that you only address array elements with the defined range. If you try and go outside of this range an exception occurs.

You can create multi dimensional arrays, although strictly speaking this is really an array of arrays:

int table[ ][ ] = new int [10][10];

You address each element in a similar way, for example:

table[3][4] = 75;

Methods

Methods describe a set of operations that can be performed on the data within a class.
To define a method you must specify:

- Modifiers - these are covered in detail in chapter 13.
- The type of the object returned by the method.
- The method name.
- The parameters passed to the object.
- The main body of the method.

To illustrate how you create and use methods, it is useful to look at a small program, with a single class and a single method:

```
class MyProgram {
    public static void main (String args[ ]) {
        System.out.println("This is MyProgram");
// display the message on the screen
    }
}
```

- The method *System.out.println* displays a string on the screen.
- All Java applications (but not applets) must have a *main* method.
- The modifiers are *public* and *static*.

Methods can be either *public* or *private*:

- A *public* method can be called from anywhere within the application.
- A *private* method can only be used within the class it is defined in.
- A *protected* method can be used anywhere it is defined.

If you do not explicitly state if a method is *public* or *private* it is given the default of *protected*.

Methods may or may not be *static*,

- Static methods have one instance per class and therefore all objects which belong to this class share the same copy of the method.
- Non static methods have one instance per object. To specify non static omit the *static* keyword.

The default is **not** *static*. This is discussed in chapter 13.

At this stage do not worry too much about modifiers, virtually all the methods you will use will be non static and *public*.

The *main* method returns a void object, other methods as you will see later may return for example, *String*, or *integer* objects.

The name of the method - *main* in this case, is next. This method is executed first in an application. Applets do not have a *main* method.

Finally the parameters of the method. These are enclosed in brackets. The single parameter is a *String* object called *args[ ]*. The *main* method is unusual in that this parameter is used to pass information to the method from the command line which starts the application running. This is covered in detail in chapter 3.

Calling methods

The next example has two classes each with a single method. The *main* method is virtually the same except for a call to the *fahrenheitToCentigrade* method, which returns a float object. If a type is not specified then the default of *integer* is used. In this case this method returns a floating point temperature using the *return* statement. If the return type is *void* then there is no value returned.

```
class MyProgram {
    public static void main (String args[ ]) {
        float centi, fahr = 67.5;
        centi = fahrenheitToCentigrade(fahr);
        System.out.println(fahr + " fahrenheit is " +centi+ " centigrade");
// display the message on the screen
        }
    }
class Temperature {
// convert the fahrenheit temperature to centigrade
    public static float fahrenheitToCentigrade(float fahrenheit) {
        return (fahrenheit - 32) * 5 / 9;
// return the temperature in centigrade
```

```
        }
    }
```

In the *fahrenheitToCentigrade* method a single floating point value is passed to the method.

Creating a class and an object

This chapter has introduced a lot of new terminology. At this stage it is helpful to look at another example where we define a class and a few methods, and create an instance of that class.

If you want to create a class and instantiate it, that is create an instance of it, the first stage is to define the class with a *class* definition:

```
class Building {
}
```

Next define the variables of the class:

```
class Building {
    int floors;        // the number of floors
    float floorArea;   // the floor area
    String use;        // work, storage, recreation, or living
}
```

Finally create the methods of the class, for example, these two methods display and change the use of the building:

```
void displayUse( ) {
    System.out.println("This building is used for" + function);
}

void changeUse(String newUse) {
    use = newUse;
}
```

The declaration of the class variables and the methods defines the class. To create an instance of the class you need the following statement to the *main* method:

```
Building b = new Building( );
```

This defines *b* as being an instance of the *Building* class.

To create an executable application you need to add a *main* method after your class definition:

```
public static void main(String args[ ]) {
    Building b = new Building( );
    b.floors = 4;
    b.floorArea = 2000;
    b.use = "work";
```

```
            b.displayUse( );
            b.changeUse("recreation");
            b.displayUse( );
      }
```

The statement:

```
      b.floors = 4;
```

assigns the number of floors of instance *b* to 4, similarly:

```
      b.floorArea = 2000;
      b.use = "work";
```

defines the floor area of *b* to *2000* and its use to *work*.
The *displayUse* method for this instance is executed using the statement:

```
      b.displayUse( )
```

If you run this application two messages will be displayed:

This building is used for work
This building is used for recreation

Instance variables

Classes have associated variables which form part of the class definition, these are declared in the same way as local variables except that they are defined outside of a method, that is directly after the *class* statement:

```
class Garage extends Building {
      int floorArea;
      Int numberOfWindows;
      String usage;
}
```

These variables are called instance variables and are global for each instance of the class.

Class variables

Class variables are defined in the same way as instance variables except that the keyword static is used:

```
      static bufferSize;
```

These are globally available throughout the class, rather than having a different variable for every instance.

Constants

A constant is a "variable" whose value is fixed at the start of the program and cannot be changed. In Java local variables cannot be constants, only instance and class variables can.

To declare a constant use the *final* keyword and specify the constant value:

> *final limit = 100;*
> *final String fileError = "File not Found";*

Class variables are usually placed after the definition of the class, adjacent to the definition of the instance variables.

Using instance variables

Class variables are available globally through the class, while instance variables are available throughout the instance. There is a straightforward syntax for using them. Specify the name of the object on the left, a dot, and then the name of the class or instance variable. In the example below the class *Garage* has 3 instance variables (they would be class variables if the keyword *static* was placed before each of their definitions):

```
public static main (String args[ ]) {
    Garage myGarage = new Garage( );
    myGarage.usage = "Junk storage";
    ....
}

class Garage extends Building {
    int floorArea;
    Int numberOfWindows;
    String usage;
}
```

An instance of the *Garage* object is created by the line:

> *Garage myGarage = new Garage( );*

The instance variable *usage* is assigned a value by the line:

> *myGarage.usage = "Junk storage";*

The other instance variables can be referenced in the same way by specifying the object name, and variable name, in this case as *myGarage.floorArea* and *myGarage.numberOfWindows*.

Using class variables

You refer to class variables in the same way as instance variables, using the dot notation:

```
class Mondeo {
    static String model = "Mondeo";
    int engineSize;
    ....
}

    ...
    Mondeo slowCar, fastCar;
    slowcar.engineSize = 1600;
    fastcar.engineSize = 2800;
    System.out.println("The model is a " + slowCar.model);
    ....
```

slowCar and *fastCar* are both different instances of the *Mondeo* class and can have different values of the instance variables *engineSize*. They must have the same value for the *model* variable since this is a class variable, that is there is only one value per class, rather than one value per instance. *slowCar.model* is always the same as *fastCar.model*.

The keyword *this*

The keyword *this* provides a useful way of referring to the current object within a method, using the dot notation. If the current object has an instance variable called *value*, you can refer to it as *this.value*

If you wish to pass the current object as a parameter, *this* provides an easy way of doing it:

```
    Initialise(this);
```

The keyword *this* can only be used within a instance method, not within a class method, since *this* refers to the current instance of a class.

Arithmetic in Java

Java has the five usual arithmetic operators shown in table 4.2.

The same operator is used for both integer and floating point division. In integer division the result is never rounded up, for example *14/5* is *2* not *3*.

The modulus operator, *%*, gives the remainder after integer division, for example *14%5* is *4*, since the remainder of *14/5* is *4*.

Table 4.2 *The arithmetic operators.*

Operator	Meaning
+	Addition.
-	Subtraction.
/	Division.
*	Multiplication.
%	Modulus.

Assigning number variables

You can assign one variable to another using the equal operator, =, as you can in most programming languages, but what happens if the variables are of different types? If you mix *int* and *float* variables the integers are converted to *float* before any calculations are carried out. Similarly if *float* and *double* variables are mixed, the *floats* are converted to *double*. In C++ jargon the weaker variables are converted to the stronger variable type. The stronger the type the wider the range of values that it can represent. Floating point variables can represent a wider range of numbers than integers and so are the stronger of the two.

```
double litre, gallon;
float mile, kilometre;

litre = gallon * 0.22;
kilometre = (mile * 5 ) / 8;
```

In the above example, the constant 0.22 is automatically a *double* quantity. The constants 5 and 8 are initially integers because they do not have a decimal point. Since kilometre is a float variable they are converted to *float* before any calculations are carried out. It would be better to put:

```
kilometre = (mile * 5.0 ) / 8.0;
```

To make it clearer that the calculation would be carried out using floating point variables.

After the calculation has been carried out the result is converted to the type of the variable on the left hand side of the assignment.

```
int centigrade, freezingPoint;
double fahrenheit;

freezingPoint = 32;
centigrade = (fahrenheit - freezingPoint) * 5.0 / 9.0;
```

In this example the strongest variable on the right side of the assignment is *fahrenheit* which is *double*. Everything is converted to *double*, the calculation is carried out and the result is converted to *int* and assigned to the variable *centigrade*.

Casting

You can rely on the default automatic conversion between the different data types that Java offers, but sometimes you want to make it clear what is happening, or you may wish to override the action that Java will take. You can do this by explicitly casting variables, that is converting one data type to another. You do this by specifying the type that you want the variable to be converted to by placing that type in brackets in front of the variable name, for example:

> *int c, d;*
> *float value;*
> *...*
> *value = (float) c / (float) d;*

This converts the *int* variables *c* and *d* into *float* variables.

You can cast an object to another object providing that they are a subclass and super class of each other.

You cannot cast an object to one of the basic data types.

Assigning characters, strings and boolean variables

To assign a single character, you enclose the character in single quotes:

> *myCharacter = 'a';*
> *myNewlineCharacter = '\n';*

There are some non printing characters that Java provides a simple way of writing, which are listed in table 4.3

Table 4.3 *The non printing characters.*

Code	Description
\n	New line.
\t	tab.
\b	Backspace.
\r	Carriage return.
\f	Formfeed.
\\	Backslash.
\'	' character.
\"	" character.
\ddd	Octal number.
\xdd	Hexadecimal number.
\udddd	Unicode character.

When you are using booleans you can assign them the values *true* and *false*, for example:

> *boolean learningJava = true;*

You assign *String* objects by enclosing the starting in double quotes:

myString = "This is a short string";

You can also use the codes for the non printable characters:

myString "Heading 1 \t Heading 2\n";

Assignment operators

Java has the usual assignment operator = that we have already seen, but in common with C++ there are some additional features to assignment.

If you want to assign more than one variable to the same value you can use expressions like the one shown below:

firstCount, secondCount, thirdCount = 0;

All of the variables are assigned the value zero.
There is also a shorthand way of writing expressions such as:

firstCount = firstCount + 7;
newValue = newValue / interval;

In the first line *firstCount* is increased by 7. In the second *newValue* is divided by *interval*. In both cases the left hand side is assigned to its current value after it has been operated on by a constant or variable. A shorthand way of rewriting these two lines is:

firstCount += 7;
newValue /= interval;

As you would expect you can also use the subtraction and multiplication operators in the same way as shown in table 4.4.

There is a special case of this type of operation, when a value is being incremented or decremented by one.

firstCount = firstCount + 1;
firstCount += 1;
firstCount++;

All three of these lines perform the same operation. You can also use:

++firstCount;

which has exactly the same effect.

Table 4.4 *Shortcut operators.*

Operation	Meaning
c += d	c = c + Delphi
c -= d	c = c - Delphi
c /= d	c = c / Delphi
c *= d	c = c * Delphi
c++	c = c + 1
c--	c = c - 1

If you want to decrease a variable by one, you can use either of these notations:

> *firstCount--;*
> *--firstCount;*

It is more common to add the operators after the variable name rather than before.

Why does Java provide these different ways of specifying the same operations? Firstly the notation is easy to use and most Java programmers feel that it provides a concise way of specifying these common operations. The second reason is that the code generated by the compiler may be different. If, for example, the ++ operator is specified this is a signal to the compiler to use the increment instruction in the assembler rather than the addition instruction. Since the increment instruction may execute several times faster than the add instruction, the program will run faster. In practice these days, a good optimising compiler can determine the most efficient instructions to use, but the notation has been used and liked by many C++ programmers and so it is reasonable to stick with it.

Assigning objects

If you want to copy the variables assigned to one object to another you can do it using the = operator, copying the values one at a time. Here is an example where there are two instances of a class which describes people's jobs and you want to copy one instance to the other - perhaps when one person takes over the job of another.

> *public void class Job {*
> *String occupation;*
> *int salary;*
> *....*
> *johnsWork Job = new Job( );*
> *pamsWork Job = new Job( );*
> *.....*
> *johnsWork.occupation = pamsWork.occupation;*
> *johnsWork.salary = pamsWork.salary:*
> *.....*
> *}*

You cannot write *johnsWork = pamsWork*. Fortunately there is a shorthand way of assigning all the instance variables of an object to another object using the *copy* method:

> *johnsWork = copy(pamsWork);*

This has the effect of copying all the instance variables assigned to *pamsWork* to *johnsWork*.

Comparison operators

Java has the usual set of operators for comparing variables:

Table 4.5 *The comparison operators.*

Operator	Meaning
==	Equal
!=	Not equal
<	Less than
>	Greater than
<=	Less than or equal to
>=	Greater than or equal to

Note the difference between the assignment operator and the equality operator:

> *if (c == d) e = f;*

This above line compares *c* and *d* and if they are equal assigns the value of *f* to *e*. The following line of code has confused these two operators and has an unexpected result:

> *if (c = d) e == f;*

This incorrect statement will not give an error message. It will assign the value of *d* to *c* and will never assign the value *f* to *e* (*e == f* is just a test for equality).

Comparing objects

You can use the == and the != operators to test if two items are the same object, but this is rather less useful than might be supposed at first. These operators do not test to see if the same values have been assigned to the two operands. If, for example, you have two different *String* objects which have the same text assigned to them they will not return a *true* value when tested for equality, unless they both refer to the same object. This can sometimes lead to confusing results.

Overloaded methods

We have looked at defining methods. One of the key things which you have to include in the method definition is a list of parameters which are passed to the method. If you attempt to call a method with an incorrect or incomplete parameter list, the Java compiler will flag an error. This is reasonable and is what you would expect, but in some circumstances it can be inconvenient if, for example, you want one of the parameters to be optional. Java allows more than one method to have the same name providing they have different parameters. When you call a method Java examines the parameters that you have provided and calls the appropriate method. This is called method overloading.

In the next example there are two methods concerned with displaying an error message.

```
class ShowError {

    ShowError reportError(String message) {
        System.out.println(message);
    }

    ShowError reportError( ) {
        System.out.println("Unspecified error occurred");
    }
}
```

If you use the call:

```
reportError( );
```

The standard error message *Unspecified error occurred* will be displayed. If you use the call:

```
reportError("File not found");
```

the specified text will be displayed.

Note that although the parameters are different the return value must be of the same type or there will be a compiler error.

You are not limited to two methods with the same name, you can have as many as you want.

Constructors

If you look at the Sun World Wide Web pages that define many Java classes, you will see the methods for the class defined, and also a heading of *Constructor Index*.

Constructors are special methods which control how an object is initialised. They cannot be called directly, but are run by Java every time a new object is created, that is every time the *new* directive is used. You can rely on the default constructors for initialising your variables and calling any other methods, or you can define your own.

A constructor method for a class always has the same name as the class, and does not have a return type.

The application shown below creates an instance of the *Country* class and will print out *The capital of England is London   The population is 52000000.*   The default constructors for the *Country* class are used, they are called implicitly by Java.

```
class Country {
    String name;
    String capital;
    int population;

    public static void main (String args[ ]) {
        Country england;

        england = new Country( );
        england.name = "England";
        england.capital = "London";
        england.population = 52000000;
        System.out.print("The capital of " + england.name);
        System.out.print(" is " + england.capital + "The population is ");
        System.out.print(england.population);
    }
}
```

You can obtain the same result by supplying your own constructor for this class:

```
class Country {
    String name;
    String capital;
    int population;

    Country(String theName, String theCapital, int thePopulation) {
        name = theName;
        capital = theCapital;
        population = thePopulation;
    }

    public static void main (String args[ ]) {
        Country england;

        england = new Country(England, London, 52000000 );
        System.out.print("The capital of " + england.name);
        System.out.print(" is " + england.capital + "The population is ");
        System.out.print(england.population);
    }
}
```

This application produces exactly the same output as the previous one. The new constructor method takes three parameters which are used to initialise the object when it is created.

You can overload constructors just as you can overload ordinary methods. If you look at the Sun World Wide Web pages you will see that this is a common procedure.

The *finalize* method

Constructor methods are created when an object is created, the *finalize* method is called when an object is destroyed, or at the end of the program whichever is the sooner. It is unlikely that you would wish to create your own *finalize* method except to optimise the garbage collection of an object, ensuring that all the resources such as memory which have been allocated to this object will be released. To create your own *finalize* method,

```
void finalize( ) {
    ...
}
```

This overrides the default method.

5

Branching and Looping

Introduction

So far all the programming examples that we have looked at consist of lines of code that are run one after another, without any looping or conditional statements. All programming languages need to be able to repeat some parts of the program more than once, and to make decisions based on the value of data. Java is no exception. If you have programmed in a high level language before you will be familiar with the concepts in this chapter, but Java does have a few unexpected features even for C++ programmers.

This chapter also looks at the remaining operators which we have not yet covered.

In this chapter you will learn about:

- *If...else* statements.
- The conditional operator.
- *Switch* statements.
- *for*, *while* and *do* loops.
- Logical and bitwise operators.

If...else statements

In common with most programming languages the *if* statements provides a way for your programs to make decisions.

> *if (memorySize < 8)*
> *System.out.println("Are things a bit slow?");*

If the integer variable *memorySize* is less than 8Mb the message will be displayed. The method *System.out.println* prints a string on the screen.

You can extend the message by using an *else* clause:

> *if (memorySize < 8)*
> *System.out.println("Perhaps you should buy more memory");*

```
else
    System.out.println("You have adequate memory");
```

You can also use multiple *else* clauses:

```
if (memorySize <= 8)
    System.out.println("Perhaps you should buy more memory");
else (if memorySize <= 16)
    System.out.println("You have adequate memory");
else
    System.out.println("You have ample memory");
```

Only one of these clauses is carried out. If the memory size is found to be less or equal to 8, the message *Perhaps you should buy more memory* is printed and the rest of the statement is skipped. If the memory is greater than 8 but equal to or less than 16 *You have adequate memory* is displayed. If neither of these conditions are met, then the memory size must be more than 16Mb or more.

You can have as many *else* clauses as you like, but more than two becomes confusing. Fortunately Java provides a better way of carrying multiple *else* statements using the *switch* and *case* statements as you will see later in this chapter.

You can have more than one test condition in *if..else* statements, for example:

```
if ((channel == 2) && (day == Sunday))
    System.out.println(" Babylon 5 on today");
```

Block statements

A useful feature that Java shares with C++ is that a set of statements can be grouped together to behave like a single statement. In an *if..else* statement, if the condition specified is met, the following line is executed, for example:

```
if (day == "Saturday")
    goShopping( );
```

Sometimes, however, you want to execute a number of lines of code if the specified condition is met. Java allows you to do this. The statements that you group together are enclosed in a { } pair, for example:

```
if (day == "Friday") {
    calculate_payroll( );
    deduct tax( );
    printPayslips( );
}
```

If the *day* is *Friday* the enclosed operations are carried out. Anywhere where you can use a single statement you can use a block statement.

The conditional operator

The conditional operator provides a shorthand way of performing some *if..else* statements. The syntax looks cryptic at first, but when you have used it a few times it will become familiar. The statements:

```
if (memory <= 8)
     message = "memory too small";
else
     message = "memory adequate";
System.out.println(message);
```

can be rewritten as:

```
string message = memory <= 8 ? "memory too small" : "memory adequate"
     System.out.println(message);
```

The general syntax is:

```
test ? true result : false result
```

If the test (in this case *memory <= 8*) is found to be *true*, the true result ("*memory too small*") is returned in the string *message*. If it is *false*, the false result ("*memory adequate*") is returned in *message*.

Switch statements

The *switch..case* provides a shorthand way of writing certain *if..else* statements. It is common in programming to test a variable against a series of values, for example:

```
if (memory == 4)
     System.out.println("More memory needed");
else (if memory == 8)
     System.out.println("Just adequate");
else (if memory == 12)
     System.out.println("Adequate memory");
else (if memory == 16)
     System.out.println("Enough memory");
```

This can be neatly replaced by the following code:

```
switch (memory)  {
     case 4:
          System.out.println("More memory needed");
          break;
     case 8:
          System.out.println("Just adequate");
          break;
     case 12:
```

```
            System.out.println("Adequate memory");
            break;
        case 16:
            System.out.println("Enough memory");
    }
```

Note that at the end of each case clause there is a *break* statement. In common with C++ if a condition is met, the associated code is executed, and the program then executes all of the code below it. If the *break* statements were not included and the memory was 4Mb, then all four messages would be printed. The *break* statements ensure that the program exits from the *switch* statements after a match has been found.

You can add a *default* clause at the end (but before the closing *}* bracket) which will have a following line of code which that will be executed if none of the case conditions are met:

```
        default: System.out.println("You have enough memory");
```

There are a few limitations on the use of this statement. You can only test for four primitive types, *byte*, *char*, *int* and *short*. You cannot use *float* or *String*, or test for any condition apart from equality. Despite these limitations this is a useful statement that should be used in preference to multiple *if..else* statements wherever possible.

Looping

Loops allow the same block of code to be repeated many times. There are three types of loops in Java. They are:

- *while* loops.
- *do..while* loops.
- *for* loops.

While loops

while loops have two parts. The body of the loop which is preceded by a condition. While the condition is met the body of the loop is executed, for example:

```
        count = 0;
        while (count < 10) {
            System.out.println("count is " + count);
            count++;
        }
```

Initially count is zero, so the body of the loop is executed. The variable count is then incremented. When the program reaches the end of the loop block of code it checks the *while* condition again and finds that count is now one - still less than 10, so the body of the loop is executed a second time. The values 0 to 9 will be displayed before this *while* loop is terminated. The condition evaluates to a boolean condition. The loop is executed repeatedly until the condition evaluates to false.

You can have multiple test conditions in *while* loops, for example:

```
count = 0;
theend = false;
while ((count < 10) && (theend == false)) {
    System.out.println("count is " + count);
    count++;
    theend = instream.read( );    // read a character
}
```

The body of the loop is only executed when the conditions are both true. Note that each of the two conditions are enclosed in parentheses and that both of them are enclosed with a further pair of parentheses.

Do..while loops

do..while loops are similar to *while* loops and in most cases they can be substituted for each other. The code below performs in a similar way to the previous example:

```
count = 0;
theend = false;
do {
    System.out.println("count is " + count);
    count++;
    theend = instream.read( );    // read a character
} while ((count < 10) && (theend == false))
```

The body of the loop is preceded by *do* and an opening parenthesis. The *while* conditions follow the closing parenthesis at the end of the block.

This code is not, however exactly the same. The values 0 to 9 will be displayed as before, but if the initial value of count was 10 this program would display the value 10. The *while* loop example would not display any value. *do..while* loops are always executed once. In some circumstances, the body of *while* loops may never be executed.

For loops

One of the most common things that programmers want to do in a loop is to increment or decrement a value, *for* loops provide a way of doing this. The *for* loop has three components followed by the loop body.

```
for (count = 0; count < 10; count++) {
    System.out.println("count is " + count);
}
```

- The first part, *count = 0*, initialises the loop, if you have a loop counter, such as *count* you can give it an initial value.
- The second part, *count < 10*, is the test condition. The body of the loop enclosed in parentheses will execute while this condition is met.
- The third part, *count++*, is an expression that is evaluated every time the body of the loop executes. While this is usually used to increment or decrement a loop counter, other expressions, for example *count += 3* could be used instead.

In the example above the parentheses enclosing the body of the loop could have been omitted, since if they are not found, the body of the loop is expected to be only one line long.

Quitting loops

Sometimes you do need to get out of a loop before it has terminated, if for example an error occurs and there is no point in continuing. You can do this using the *break* and *continue* statements. In the example below, a character is read and tested to see if it is a new line character '\n'. If it is, the program jumps out of the loop.

```
do {
    newchar = instream.read( ); // read a character
    if (newchar == '\n') break;
    System.out.println("count is " + count);
    count++;
} while ((count < 10))
```

If the *continue* statement is used rather than break, the program will ignore the rest of the loop body, and go to the start of the loop again.

If you have nested loops, *break* only exits the current loop, you need a break statement for every loop or to use labelled loops. At the start of the nested loops that you want to exit put a label and add the name of the label, *errorFound*, after *break*. In the example below, characters are read and displayed fifty characters to the line for a maximum of ten lines. If one of the input characters is a null '\0' then both loops are terminated and the message *The end* is displayed.

```
errorFound:
    for (c=0; c< 10; c++){
        for (c = 0; c< 50; c++) {
            newchar = instream.read( );  // read a character
            if (newchar == '\0') break errorFound;
            System.out.print(newchar);
        }
        System.out.println("");
        count++;
    }
    System.out.println("The end");
```

It does not matter how many nested loops there are or if they are of different types.

Java operators

So far we have only looked at the assignment operators, but Java offers a wide range of operators, all the ones you would expect, plus a few surprises. Even if you are an experienced high level language programmer it is worthwhile reviewing this section to make sure that you are aware of all the operators which Java offers. In particular the way in which Java operates on strings is very different to C++.

Bitwise operators

All data in computers is stored as a sequence of binary data or bits, for example the decimal number 145 can be written in 8 bits as 10010001 as shown below.

128	64	32	16	8	4	2	1		
1	0	0	1	0	0	0	1	=	128+16+1=145

The bitwise operators work with the corresponding pairs of bits in two variables rather than on the values as a whole.

Java offers all the bitwise operators from C++.

Table 5.1 The bitwise operators.

Operator	Meaning
&	Bitwise AND.
|	Bitwise OR.
^	Bitwise XOR.
<<	Left shift.
>>	Right shift.
>>>	Zero fill right shift
~	Bitwise complement.
<<=	Left shift assignment.
>>=	Right shift assignment.
>>>=	Zero fill, right shift assignment.
&=	AND assignment.
|=	AND assignment.
^=	XOR assignment.

These operators are not commonly used, but they do reflect origins in C++ as a language which is able to deal with low level operations at the bit level.

These bitwise operations can be explained by using truth tables. For example the truth table for the bitwise operator & is:

Table 5.2 *The & operator.*

A	B	A & B
0	0	0
0	1	0
1	0	0
1	1	1

The & operator works on pairs of bits. Since a bit can either be 0 or 1 the truth table is able to show the output from the & operator for all the possible pairs of inputs. There are 4 possible inputs, 00, 01, 10 and 11. The third column in the table shows the output from these pairs of inputs. The & operator is applied to all pairs of corresponding bits in the variables concerned. For example 27 & 134. 27 in binary is 0000 0000 0001 1011. 134 in binary is 0000 0000 0100 0011.

$$
\begin{array}{ll}
\text{0000 0000 0001 1011} & \\
\underline{\text{0000 0000 0100 0011}} & \underline{\&} \\
\text{0000 0000 0000 0011} &
\end{array}
$$

The result of applying the & operator is 0000 0000 0000 0011 in binary which is 3 in decimal.

Similarly the truth table for the bitwise *or* operator | is:

Table 5.3 *The | operator.*

A	B	A	B
0	0	0
0	1	1
1	0	1
1	1	1

27 | 134 is given by:

$$
\begin{array}{ll}
\text{0000 0000 0001 1011} & \\
\underline{\text{0000 0000 0100 0011}} & \underline{\quad | \quad} \\
\text{0000 0000 0101 1011} & 91
\end{array}
$$

The truth table for the bitwise *xor* operator ^ is:

Table 5.4 *The ^ operator.*

A	B	A ^ B
0	0	0
0	1	1
1	0	1
1	1	0

27 ^ 134 is given by:

```
0000 0000 0001 1011
0000 0000 0100 0011      ^
0000 0000 0101 1000      88
```

The shift operators move the whole pattern of bits either to the left or the right. For example, 18 in binary is 0000 0000 0001 0010. 18 >> 1 moves the bit pattern one place to the right to give 0000 0000 0000 1001 = 9. 18 << 3 moves the bit pattern three places to the left to give 0000 0000 1001 0000 = 144.

Shifting the bit pattern of a variable one place to the right has the same effect as dividing the variable by 2. Shifting two places to the right divides by 4, three places divides by 8 and so on.

Shifting the bit pattern to the left, multiplies the variable in the same way.

The assignment operators in this group simply provide a useful shorthand notation, for example:

value = value << 3

has the same effect as:

value <<= 3.

The bit pattern of *value* is shifted three places to the left, effectively a multiplication by 2^3 (=8).

Logical operators

Some operations result in a boolean value, that is either a *true* or *false* value, for example:

If (c == d) newValue = oldValue;

The test for equality between *c* and *d* gives a boolean value of *true* if they are equal and *false* if they are not. When a *true* value is found, the assignment *newValue = oldValue* is carried out. Sometimes it is useful to combine tests like this:

if ((c == d) && (e == f)) newValue = oldValue;

In this example, only if both *(c == d)* and *(e == f)* give boolean values of *true* is *newValue* assigned to *oldValue*. The left expression (c == d) is evaluated first and if it is found to be *false*, the right expression *(e == f)* is not evaluated. If you substitute the operator & for && then both the right and left expressions will be evaluated regardless of the value of the first expression evaluated. It is usual in Java programming to use the && operator and difficult to think of situations where & should be used in preference.

Similarly the *or* operators | and || are used with a pair of expressions which yield boolean results, for example:

if (c == d) || (e == f) newValue = oldValue;

If either *(c == d)* or *(e == f)* or both give boolean values of *true* the *newValue* is assigned to *oldValue*.

If the *xor* operator ^ is used in place of the | or || operator it will carry out the assignment if either *(c == d)* or *(e == f)* gives a *true* value, but not if both give a true value.

if ((engineSize>2000) || (age < 21)) then highInsurance( );

In the above example, the || operator is the correct one to use, since a high insurance premium should be charged if either or both of the conditions are met.

The full set of logical operators is given below.

Table 5.5 *The logical operators.*

Operator	Meaning
&	AND, both left and right sides evaluated.
&&	AND right side only evaluated if left side == *true*.
|	OR, both left and right sides evaluated.
||	OR, right side only evaluated if left side == *true*
^	XOR.
!	NOT.

The NOT operator ! is different from the other operators in that it requires only a single expression. If the expression evaluates to true this operator changes it to false and vice versa. The two expressions below have the same effect, but the first one is much clearer:

if age >= 18 voter( );
if !(age < 18) voter ( );

Operator precedence

When a sequence of mathematical operations is carried out, the order in which this is done can be very important, for example:

c = 9 + 6 / 3;

If the addition is carried out first the expression becomes 15/3 = 5. If the division is done first, it becomes 9+2 = 11. In this case the division would be done first, since the division operator has a higher precedence than the addition operator. The operators, in order of precedence, are listed in table 5.6. If you are in doubt, or want to make it clear to another programmer who looks at your code later what the precedence is, it is a good idea to use parentheses, since operations in parentheses are always carried out first, for example:

average = (value1 + value2 + value3) / 3;

Table 5.6 Operator precedence.

Operator	Meaning
( ) [ ] .	Parentheses. The . operator accesses methods and variables.
++ -- ! ~	Increment, decrement, not, complement.
New	Creates a new instance of a class.
* / %	Multiplication, division, modulus.
+ -	Addition and subtraction.
<< >> >>>	left and right shift.
< > <= >=	Less than, greater than.
== !=	Equal to, not equal to.
&	Bitwise AND.
^	Bitwise XOR.
|	Bitwise OR.
&&	Logical AND.
||	Logical OR.
= += -= /= %= ^= &= |= <<= >>= >>>=	Assignments.

When operators have the same precedence, the leftmost one is carried out first.

Using strings in Java

One of the chief complaints of C++ programmers is the way in which strings are handled. In C++ strings are arrays of characters terminated by a null character. It is not possible to add strings together as it is in languages such as Visual Basic where it is possible to concatenate strings using the + or the & operators. This problem has been dealt with very successfully in Java. Strings are sequences of characters, and are instances of the class *String*, which has an associated set of methods that perform many of the standard string operations that you are likely to use, for concatenating or amending strings.

Strings can be defined just as if they were one of the basic types such as *float*, for example:

```
String best, worst;

best = " Java ";
worst = " COBOL "
System.out.println("I prefer" + best + " to " + worst);
```

This code will print out the text *I prefer Java to COBOL* on the screen.
An equivalent way of doing this is:

```
String best, worst, myPreferences;

best = " Java ";
worst = " COBOL "
myPreferences = "I prefer" + best + " to " + worst;
System.out.println(myPreferences);
```

You can also use the += operator with strings, for example:

```
String best, worst, myPreferences;

best = " Java ";
worst = " COBOL "
myPreferences = "I prefer";
myPreferences += best + "to"
myPreferences += worst;
System.out.println(myPreferences);
```

This will print out the same string.

6
Graphics

Introduction

Graphics help to bring a dull applet or Web page to life. One of the first uses of Java was to add animation to Web pages to make them look more interesting. If this was the only use of Java it would be worthwhile, but graphics are an invaluable way of expressing information. Reading a description of a fractal is dull and mathematical, but if you see fractals being drawn it quickly becomes clear what they are. Lists of figures which are tedious to interpret are greatly helped by drawing a graph or chart.

Sun, the developers of Java, anticipated that software developers would want to make extensive use of graphics and so Java was developed with a powerful library of classes to allow you to draw your own pictures, to import images and to create animation.

In this chapter you will learn how to:

- Draw basic shapes.
- Change the font and size of text.
- Change the colour of your images.
- Display existing images.

Graphics basics

In Java, packages are collections of classes which have a related function. One of these packages provides a set of classes which deal with graphics.

The basic graphics and text drawing methods are implemented in the *Graphics* class, which is part of the *java.awt* package. To access any of the graphics methods you must import the *Graphics* class by adding the following *import* statement at the start of your file.:

    import java.awt.Graphics

With other classes you would usually create an instance of the class so that you can use it. In the case of the *Graphics* class you automatically have an instance of the graphics class available for use within your applets via the *paint* method:

public void paint (Graphics g){

        ....

}

Graphics drawing commands are normally placed in the *paint* method and these methods make use of the graphics object *g*. This will become clearer as you read through this chapter. The best way to learn any programming language is to try some examples. The examples are particularly satisfying when learning how to use graphics, since you can immediately see if your applet has worked correctly.

The methods for drawing graphics use a co-ordinate system. The co-ordinate system has the origin (0, 0) at the top left of the drawing area. Moving to the right is a positive x movement. Moving down the screen is a positive movement in the y direction. The drawing methods use x and y values to represent the start and end points of the object to be drawn, with the x value representing points across the screen and the y value representing points down the screen. To draw a line from the 0,0 position to 199,99 as shown in fig. 6.1 you use the *drawLine* method, which is called from the *paint* method:

public void paint (Graphics g) {
        g.drawLine (0, 0, 199, 99);
}

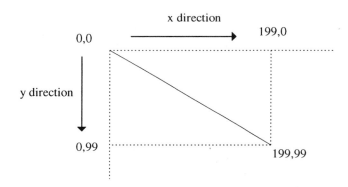

Fig. 6.1 *The graphics co-ordinate system.*

Co-ordinates are specified as integer values, that is they must be whole positive numbers.

The size of the drawing area is set by specifying the HEIGHT and WIDTH parameters in the HTML document. For example, the HTML code that creates a drawing area of 200 pixels wide by 100 pixels deep would be :

<HTML>
<HEAD>
<TITLE>Simple Graphics Example</TITLE>
</HEAD>
<BODY>
<APPLET CODE="MySimpleGraphics.class" WIDTH=200 HEIGHT=100>

A simple graphics example ...
</APPLET>
</BODY>
</HTML>

Graphics drawing methods

There are several methods in the *java.awt.Graphics* package for drawing basic shapes such as lines, rectangles and arcs. In the examples in this chapter you will see that all the drawing methods are specified as *g.drawLine* or *g.drawRect*. The 'g' is an instance of the *graphics* class and the drawing methods are defined as part of that class. Most drawing commands tend to be placed in the *paint* method which supplies an instance of the Graphics object for us to use:

> *public void paint (Graphics g) {*
>   ....
> *}*

Lines and points

You have already seen an example of the use of the *drawLine* method. The method takes four parameters - the x and y co-ordinates for the start and end points of the line. In the example below, a line will be drawn from co-ordinates (5, 35) to (75, 35) - a horizontal line:

> *g.drawLine (5, 35, 75, 35);*

There is no method for drawing a single point but you can use the *drawLine* method to achieve this by using the same start and end co-ordinates, for example:

> *g.drawLine (10, 25, 10, 25);*

Rectangles

There are several methods provided to display rectangles. The methods share some basic characteristics:

- They all use the same basic 4 parameters to define position and size:

> *g.drawRect (startX, startY, width, height);*

- The colour used to draw and fill the rectangle is the current colour (set using the *g.setColor* method as described later in this chapter).

Plain rectangles

You can draw a simple rectangle with the *drawRect* method as shown in fig. 6.2:

> *g.drawRect (125, 35, 50, 50);*

   Fig. 6.2 *The drawRect Method.*

To create a filled rectangle use the *fillRect* method. The filled rectangle is filled with the current colour as shown in fig. 6.3:

> *g.fillRect (125, 105, 50, 50);*

   Fig. 6.3 *The fillRect Method.*

Rounded rectangles

If you want to give your rectangles a rounded corner you can use the *drawRoundRect* method. This method has an additional two parameters which specify how far from the corner of the rectangle the curve starts. The first of these two parameter specifies how far along the horizontal edge the curve should start, and the second of them how far along the vertical edge. By varying these two parameters you can get different curvature effects. The general form of the method is:

> *g.drawRoundRect (startX, startY, width, height, curveX, curveY);*

This is shown in fig. 6.4:

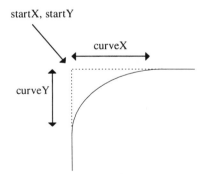   **Fig. 6.4** *The drawRoundRect method.*

The same curvature is applied to every corner. The rounded corner rectangle produced by the following line is shown in fig. 6.5:

g.drawRoundRect (250, 35, 60, 50, 25, 20);

Fig. 6.5 *Using the drawRoundRect method.*

If you want to have your rounded rectangle filled with the current colour use the *fillRoundRect* method, for example:

g.fillRoundRect (250, 245, 50, 50, 20, 20);

3D-effect rectangles

The *draw3DRect* method will produce 3-dimensional effect rectangles. In addition to the standard *startX*, *startY*, *width* and *height* co-ordinates an additional boolean parameter specifies whether the 3D-effect should make the rectangle looked raised or sunken. Specify *true* if you want a raised effect, and *false* for a sunken effect.

In the examples below, note that 3 calls have been made to the drawing method. This is because there is no ability to specify the thickness of the rectangle frame, consequently to achieve a reasonable 3D effect you will need to draw 3 or 4 rectangles inside of each other,

g.draw3DRect (375, 175, 50, 50, true);
g.draw3DRect (376, 176, 48, 48, true);
g.draw3DRect (377, 177, 46, 46, true);

Fig. 6.6 *The draw3DRect method : raised surface.*

To produce the effect of a pressed button:

g.draw3DRect (375, 245, 50, 50, false);
g.draw3DRect (376, 246, 48, 48, false);
g.draw3DRect (377, 247, 46, 46, false);

Fig. 6.7 *The draw3DRect method : sunken surface.*

Polygons

Polygons are shapes with three or more sides of different lengths. Rectangles and squares are special sorts of polygons. You specify how many sides you want by the number of co-ordinates you give. You can specify the co-ordinates of the sides either:

- As two arrays of integers (one array for x-co-ordinates and one for y-co-ordinates).
- By using the *Polygon* class.

To use the array of integers method of drawing a polygon you need to define two arrays of integers to store the x and y co-ordinates as in the example below. Note the use of the *length* method used to determine the number of elements in the arrays. This method is probably best suited to use where the co-ordinates of the shape you are drawing are fixed and known at coding time.

```
public void paint (Graphics g) {
    int xCoords[ ] = {10, 95, 175, 150, 75, 100, 10};
    int yCoords[ ] = {10, 35, 100, 150, 120, 75, 10};
    int numberCoords;
    numberCoords = xCoords.length;
    g.drawPolygon (xCoords, yCoords, numberCoords);
}
```

This code produces the polygon shown in fig. 6.8:

Fig. 6.8 *The drawPolygon method: using an array of points.*

The second method of drawing a polygon uses the *Polygon class*. To use this class you need to create an instance of the class and then you add the co-ordinates using the *addPoint* method. The code example below shows the same diamond shape drawn using this method. It also demonstrates the use of the *fillPolygon* method (we could just as easily have used the *drawPolygon* method). Note that at the top of the program you will need to include the statement to import the *Polygon* class:

```
import.awt.Polygon
public void paint (Graphics g) {
    polygon diamond = new Polygon ( );
    diamond.addPoint (85, 10);
    diamond.addPoint (160, 85);
    diamond.addPoint (85, 160);
    diamond.addPoint (10, 85);
    fillPolygon (diamond);
```

Fig. 6.9 *The drawPolygon method : using the Polygon class.*

You can have both outline and filled versions of the polygon drawing methods. The *fillPolygon* method has the advantage that it will close-up the polygon shape if the co-ordinates do not already do so. If you compare the co-ordinates defined in the two 'diamond-drawing' examples you will see that the filled diamond has one less set of co-ordinates.

Ovals

The *drawOval* and *fillOval* methods are usually used to draw circles but they can also be used to draw egg-shaped objects. The technique used to draw an oval is very similar to that for drawing a rectangle. You define the shape of the oval by constructing a rectangular container using a starting x and y co-ordinate, and width and height parameters.

To draw a circle, for example, you would define a square container as shown in fig. 6.10.

  g.drawOval (25, 25, 100, 100);

Fig. 6.10 *The drawOval method : drawing a circle.*

The second example shows a more egg-shaped oval which is filled in using the *fillOval* method. The egg-shape is achieved by having a greater height than width.

  g.fillOval (150, 25, 100, 150);

Fig. 6.11 *The drawPolygon method : drawing an oval.*

Arcs

Arcs are sections of ovals. They can be outlines or filled in using the *drawArc* and *fillArc* methods. They are drawn in a similar fashion to ovals in that their basic shape is determined by a rectangular area. In addition, the start and end points of the arc need to be provided.

The start and end points of the arc are defined in terms of the degrees in a circle. The start point is specified by a position in degrees. The end point is defined by the number of degrees to draw the arc relative to the starting point. To draw arcs in a clockwise direction you would specify a negative arc length, and a positive arc length for an anti-clockwise direction. Fig 6.12 shows the layout of the 360 degree circle.

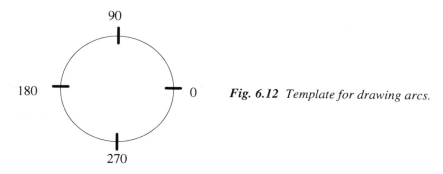

Fig. 6.12 *Template for drawing arcs.*

Figs 6.13 and 6.14 show examples of the *drawArc* method. Remember that the first four parameters specify the starting co-ordinates and size of the rectangular area the arc will be drawn in. The fifth parameter specifies that the start of the arc is at 45 degrees as shown in fig 6.13 which is analogous to a NE point on a compass. The sixth and final parameter specifies that the arc should be drawn through 135 degrees. Since this is a positive value the arc is drawn in an anticlockwise direction ending up at the 180 degree position (or NW using the compass analogy).

> *g.drawArc (25, 25, 200, 200, 45, 135);*

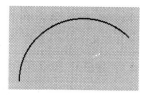

Fig. 6.13 *Drawing curves.*

The second *drawArc* example, shown in fig 6.14, demonstrates two differences. The first is the use of the *fillArc* method. A filled arc resembles a pie slice - lines are assumed to originate from the centre of the oval that the arc is part of and join up with the endpoints of the arc. The encompassed area is then filled in. Note that the length of the arc is specified as a negative figure, this means that the arc is drawn in a clockwise fashion from its starting point.

g.fillArc (25, 25, 200, 200, 45, -90);

Fig. 6.14 *Drawing pie shapes.*

Colour

No discussion of graphics routines would be complete without the use of colour. In Java, colour is supported with a *Color* class with its own methods and some methods from the *Graphics* and *Applet* classes.

Colours in Java are defined using the popular RGB model, a colour is defined by the amount of Red, Green and Blue (RGB) colour present. Each of the Red, Green and Blue components can be specified in the range of 0 to 255 (which can be represented in 8 bits or 1 byte). Since we have 3 colour elements this gives us 3 x 8 bits i.e. 24- bit colour which translates into approximately $2^{24} = 16.7$ million colours!

Bear in mind that the range of colours that your computer can display may well be a lot less than 256 colours. This will depend on the graphics card and its current mode or setting in your computer. This is an important point to remember when designing applets in Java - do not use too many colours or some of your potential users may not be able to see the full effect of your design. Remember that your applet may be run on virtually any type of computer and not everyone has a 24-bit graphics card.

Pre-defined colour

The *Color* class provides some basic pre-set colours for immediate use. These are detailed in table 6.1. The table illustrates further how the red, green and blue components are mixed to give other colours. White, for example, is made up of the maximum amount of red, green and blue, while black has no red, green or blue as shown in table 6.1.

Colours such as black and white are normally part of the default colour sets used by virtually all computer systems, using these colours you can be almost certain that your applets will be displayed as you intended.

Table 6.1 *Predefined colour variables available from the Color class.*

Colour	Red value	Green value	Blue value
Color.white	255	255	255
Color.black	0	0	0
Color.lightGray	192	192	192
Color.gray	128	128	128
Color.darkGray	64	64	64
Color.red	255	0	0
Color.green	0	255	0
Color.blue	0	0	255
Color.yellow	255	255	0
Color.magenta	255	0	255
Color.cyan	0	255	255
Color.pink	255	175	175
Color.orange	255	200	0

Defining colours

It is convenient to use the standard colours provided by the *Color* class, but sometimes you want to produce your own colours, by specifying the red, green and blue components.

> *Color myColor = new Color(200, 50, 50);*

This creates a *myColor*, which is mainly red with a hint of blue and green.

The value of each of the parameters is between 0 and 255, with 255 being the most intense. Alternatively you can use three floating point values between 0 and 1.0 which hav the same effect:

> *Color myColor = new Color(0.78, 0.20, 0.20);*

Changing object colours

Before drawing an object you have to change the colour if you do not want the default (black) to be used, you do this using the *setColor* method:

> *g.setColor(Color.blue);*

If you have defined your own colour you can specify this instead:

> *g.setColor(myColor);*

All objects drawn will have this colour until it is changed. The *setColor* method does not affect any existing objects which have been drawn. If you want to change the colour of all existing objects use the *setForeground* method:

setForeground(Color.red)

If you want to change the background colour the *setBackground* method is used:

setBackground(Color.pink);

The chameleon applet displays the text *Chameleon* 20 times, with a random size, colour and position. The *random* method is used, which produces a double length floating point value between 0 and 1.
The output from the applet is shown in fig. 6.15.

Fig. 6.15 *The Chameleon applet.*

- The size is set up first after defining the font by using the *setFont* method. It is assigned a value between 0 and 50.
- The colour is assigned using the *Color* method, each of the three components are assigned values between 0 and 1.
- The string is drawn in a random position using the *drawString* method. The x position is between 0 and *xLimit* and 0 and *yLimit* for the y position.

The complete *paint* method is shown below:

```
public void paint(Graphics g) {
    float red, green, blue;
    int c, x, y, size;
    int xLimit = 400;
    int yLimit = 300;
    Color myColor;

    for (c = 0; c < 20; c++) {
        size = (int)(Math.random( ) * 50);
        Font theFont = new Font("TimesRoman", Font.PLAIN, size);
        g.setFont(theFont);
        red = (float)Math.random( );
        green = (float)Math.random( );
```

```
                    blue = (float)Math.random( );
                    myColor = new Color(red, green, blue);
                    x = (int)(Math.random( ) * xLimit);
                    y = (int)(Math.random( ) * yLimit);
                    g.setColor(myColor);
                    g.drawString("Chameleon", x, y);
                    }
            }
    }
```

Text and fonts

Whenever you draw text on the screen the current font is used. You can change the font by using the *setFont* method. You draw text using the *drawString* method.

To create a new font, you need to specify the name of the font, whether it is bold, italic, plain or some combination of these, and the size of the characters, for example:

>   *Font theFont = new Font("TimesRoman", Font.PLAIN, 30);*

defines a plain Times Roman font with a size of 30. To assign the current font to the new font use the *setFont* method.

>   *g.setFont(theFont);*

Finally to display text use the *drawString* method.

>   *g.drawString("TimesRoman - plain", 50, 50);*

The following *paint* method displays three different fonts.

```
    public void paint(Graphics g) {
        Font theFont = new Font("TimesRoman", Font.PLAIN, 30);
        g.setFont(theFont);
        g.drawString("TimesRoman - plain", 50, 50);

        theFont = new Font("Courier", Font.BOLD, 30);
        g.setFont(theFont);
        g.drawString("Courier - bold", 50, 100);

        theFont = new Font("Arial", Font.ITALIC, 30);
        g.setFont(theFont);
        g.drawString("Arial - italic", 50, 150);
    }
```

The result is shown in figure 6.16.
You can assign a font to both italic and bold:

>   *theFont = new Font("Arial", Font.ITALIC + Font.BOLD, 30);*

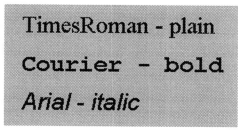

Fig. 6.16 *Displaying different fonts.*

The *getFontList* method is intended to return the names of all the available fonts, however in the latest version of Java there seems to be a bug and this method does not function correctly.

There are some useful methods for working with fonts:

Table 6.2 *Methods for working with fonts.*

Method	Description
getName( )	Returns the name of the font.
getSize( )	Gets the size of the font.
getStyle( )	Gets the style of the font - that is plain, bold or italic. A value of 0 indicates plain, 1 is bold, 2 is italic, 3 is bold and italic.
isBold( )	Returns true if the font is bold.
isItalic( )	Returns true if the font is italic.
isPlain( )	Returns true is the font is plain.

Using images

The methods we have looked at allow you to construct simple pictures, but if you want to produce professional looking applets you will need to import existing images. In Java images are not a part of the same file as your Java class files, they are stored in their own files.

Java only supports GIF and JPEG images.

The *getImage* method in the *Applet* class loads the image from a file and creates an instance of the *Image* class, for example:

Image MyImage = getImage(new URL(http://www.server.com/dmu/coffee.gif"));

One problem with specifying the location of the gif file directly is that Java is specifically designed to be system independent, it is against the whole philosophy of the language to hard code references to specification locations.

A better way of specifying the location of the file - if it is in the same directory as your Java class file or your HTML file - is to use one of the following two methods:

- *getCodeBase* returns the directory that the applet is in.
- *getDocumentBase* returns the directory that the HTML file is in.

If the file referenced above is in the same directory as the applet, the following code would be an improvement:

> *image MyImage = getImage(getDocumentBase( ), coffee.gif);*

Similarly if the image is in the same file as the HTML file:

> *image MyImage = getImage(getCodeBase( ), coffee.gif);*

If the file is not found the *getImage* method returns a null value. This does not cause an error, but the image is not displayed.

The *getImage* method does not display the image. To do this you need to use the *drawImage* method.

The *drawImage* method

There are two versions of the *drawImage* method. The first has four parameters, for example:

> *g.drawImage(coffee, 0, 0, this);*

This draws the image called coffee with the top left corner at location 0,0. It retains its original size.

If you want to specify the size, you can introduce a further two parameters, for example:

> *g.drawImage(coffee, 0, 0, 200, 200, this);*

This draws the image in the same position, but with an x and y dimension of 200 by 200. You can alter the aspect ratio of the image as shown in fig. 6.17, where the same image is drawn three times in different positions with different sizes.

The code required to produce these images is shown below.

```
import java.awt.*;
public class image extends java.applet.Applet {
Image coffee;

public void init( ) {
    setBackground(Color.white);
    coffee = getImage(getCodeBase( ),"coffee.gif");
}

public void paint(Graphics g) {
    g.drawImage(coffee, 0, 0, 200, 200, this);
    g.drawImage(coffee, 250, 0, 100, 200, this);
    g.drawImage(coffee, 210, 210, 100, 50, this);
}
}
```

Note the use of the *getCodeBase* method, which ensures that the applet looks for the image in the same directory as the class file.

Fig. 6.17 Displaying images.

The keyword *this*

In both the *getCodeBase* and *getDocumentBase* methods, the final parameter is *this*. The *this* keyword refers to the current object. It can be used wherever you wish to refer to that object.

7
Animation and Multithreading

Introduction

One of the problems of using the World Wide Web is that it can take a long time to download information, particularly for large files. Fortunately, you do not have to wait for the whole of the file to be downloaded before you can view the first part of it, or use the HTML links to view another part of the document. You can also start downloading many other pages at the same time. When your computer is waiting for data to reach it from the network, it spends most of its time not doing any useful, productive work, even when downloading many pages it is still idle most of the time. Your computer can only seem to do more than one thing at once due to multithreading, which allows applications and applets to follow different "threads of control". Multithreading is a key feature of most current professional applications, and as you would expect Java allow you to write multithreaded applications.

One of the most common uses of Java is to provide animation of images, but you need to use multithreaded code to achieve animation.

In this chapter you will learn:

- What multithreaded code is.
- How to create multiple threads.
- The problems of using multiple threads.
- How to schedule different threads.
- How to create animation.
- Techniques for reducing animation flicker.

Multithreading

Computers are able to switch rapidly between processes to give the impression to each process that it has the full resources of the computer. Many of the jobs that a computer does such as downloading World Wide Web pages or reading from a disk file are very slow relative to the speed of the computer. In these situations your computer spends most of its time just waiting for the network or the disk to provide it with the data it wants. This idea has been used for many years to allow time sharing, that is many users are able to share the same computer with each of the users' jobs being allocated successive chunks or quantums of time. Providing that there are not too many users, the time which would otherwise be wasted waiting for data to be supplied will be used for something worthwhile. This idea has been used in most browsers such as Netscape where you can request many pages to be downloaded at the same time. Each of these down-loadings is handled by a separate thread. The first page is downloaded first and you can view it while another thread carries on loading the rest of the file in the background. When you use a word processor you can be editing, while another thread is re-paginating the document in the background, or printing the file. In the PC environment, multithreading is a relatively new concept in software design, but has quickly become accepted as the preferred way of developing applications for Windows 95.

Creating new threads

There are two ways of creating threads depending on whether you want the thread to be a subclass of *java.lang.Thread* or another class.

First we are going to look at subclassing *java.lang.Thread*. To do this:

```
public class myThread extends Thread {
....
}
```

- The *run* method of this class contains the body of the thread where the bulk of the activity of the thread is carried out.
- The *start* method of the thread is called before the *run* method and carries out any initialisation. You start the thread running by calling the *start* method which automatically calls the *run* method.
- To stop the thread you use the *stop* method.
- You can also temporarily pause and restart the execution of a thread using the *suspend* and *resume* methods.

You create an instance of a thread in the same way you create an instance of any class, by using *new*:

```
myThread myT = new myThread( );    // instantiate the class
myT.start( );                      // start the thread
```

The application below shows how to create two threads. The *getName* method is used to display the name of the current thread:

```
public class MultiThreads extends Thread {
    public static void main(String args[ ]) {
    MultiThreads myT1 = new MultiThreads( );
    myT1.start( );
    MultiThreads myT2 = new MultiThreads( );
```

```
myT2.start( );
}

public void run( ) {
while (true)
    System.out.println("Thread+Thread.currentThread().getName( ));
}
}
```

This displays the text:

```
Thread-1
Thread-1
Thread-2
Thread-2
Thread-1
.....
```

The first thread was assigned the name *-1*, and the second *-2*. You would expect the threads to run alternately, but initially it is surprising to see that the application does not print out:

```
Thread-1
Thread-2
Thread-1
Thread-2
.....
```

What is happening, is that the operating system on your computer is allocating some time for the first thread to run, this is sufficient for the *while* loop to execute twice (on my computer!). This thread is then suspended and the second thread runs for a brief time, sufficient for the *while* loop to be executed a further two times, but this time in the second thread. It may print out the message from each thread a different number of times on your computer, depending on the operating system and processor you are using. To appreciate what is really going on we need to look at how Java works with the operating system of your computer.

Pre-emptive scheduling

When you have just one thread running on your computer, the operating system can allocate all the computer's resources to that thread. If you have more than one thread the resources of the computer have to be split between the different threads. This is the responsibility of the scheduler of the operating system. The operating system on most computers that Java runs on, use a type of scheduling called pre-emptive. This includes Windows 95, in fact one of the main internal differences between Windows 3.1 and Windows 95 is the scheduling technique used. The scheduling method used is a feature of your computer's operating system not of Java. Since Java can be run on a huge range of platforms it is a credit to the designers of Java and the browsers that the multithreading capabilities of Java work so well.

In pre-emptive scheduling a thread can be in one of three states:

- Running. The thread is actually being given CPU time by the computer and is executing.
- Ready. The thread is ready and able to run, but has been temporarily suspended by the operating system.
- Blocked, sometimes called waiting. The thread is not ready to run until something else happens, for example it is waiting for input from a disk or the network, or for another thread to take some action.

The transitions between these three states is shown in fig. 7.1.

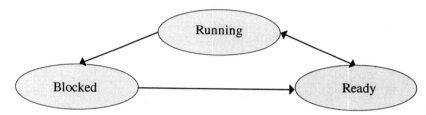

Fig. 7.1 *Thread states in a pre-emptive operating system.*

Only one thread is running at a time, assuming that you only have one processor on your computer. If you have a parallel, or multi processor computer more than one thread can be running at once. When the operating system's scheduler decides that it has allocated enough time to a running thread, it puts that thread into the ready state. It then looks at the list of threads in the ready state. All of these threads are ready and willing to run. It chooses one, usually the one which has not been run for the longest time, puts it into the running state and starts executing it. Sometimes, before a thread has used up the time that the scheduler allocates to it, it finds that it has to wait, for example, for some information to come in from the network. In this situation the thread goes into the blocked state and the scheduler chooses another thread (which is in the ready state) to run. When the information from the network has arrived, the thread in the blocked state is transferred to the ready state indicating that it is ready to run.

The amount of time allocated to each thread by the scheduler has a big impact on the performance of the computer, and some computers such as VAXs have very complicated algorithms and will allocate different amounts of time to different threads depending on what the threads are doing.

The decision on which of the threads in the ready state is to run next is also not always a straightforward one. All threads are not equal, some may need a higher priority than others.

The alternative scheduling algorithm to pre-emptive is non pre-emptive. In this system, a thread runs until it decides that it has had enough time. It then tells the operating system, which starts to run another thread. This can work satisfactorily, providing every thread manages itself well and allows other threads a fair chance to run. As you would expect this does not always happen. Windows 3.1 used non-pre-emptive scheduling, and it was a major improvement to introduce pre-emptive scheduling in Windows 95. Fortunately, virtually all computers that Java applets will run on use pre-emptive scheduling.

There is a huge amount of theory behind the way in which schedulers work which is beyond the scope of this book, but it is important to know in overview what is going on in the background when you are using multiple threads, as some unexpected and baffling things can happen if you do not know about scheduling.

Problems with multiple threads

The next application is similar to the previous one. Two instances of the same class are instantiated. The *run* method looks as if it has an error:

```
public class MultiThreads extends Thread {
static int myValue;
    public static void main(String args[ ]) {
        MultiThreads myT1 = new MultiThreads( );
        myT1.start( );
        MultiThreads myT2 = new MultiThreads( );
        myT2.start( );
    }

    public void run( ) {
    while (true) {
        myValue = 0;
        myValue++;
        if (myValue == 0) System.out.println("value is "+ myValue);
        }
    }
}
```

In the *run* method, the class variable *myValue* is assigned the value 0. It is then incremented to 1. A test is made to see if it is 0 and if it is, a message is displayed. It would seem impossible that the message could ever be displayed. In fact when the application is run it displays the message:

value is 0

about once a second. What is going on?

The first instance runs and assigns *myValue* to 0, then increments it to 1. At this moment, the scheduler may stop the first instance and start the second instance running. This assigns *myValue* to 0. At this point it is stopped by the scheduler and the first instance runs again. It tests *myValue* and finds that it is 0, since it has just been assigned to 0 by the second instance, and displays the message. While this does depend on the two instances being interrupted at precise moments it happens sufficiently often to occur about one per second in this application.

Instances have their own local variables, but share class variables, which can cause problems in situations like the one described where more than one thread is changing and reading the same variables. It is easy to spot the problem in this example, but it is possible to have more complicated applications where a subtle problem like this occurs perhaps once every few weeks. The users are surprised that something has gone wrong, perhaps the applet crashes or gives incorrect answers. The problem cannot be repeated easily since it depends on the precise interaction between multiple threads, which may only occur infrequently. Software bugs which are not repeatable can be almost impossible to find, so use any data which is shared between multiple threads with care. Fortunately Java provides a solution to this problem that you should use when designing your applets and applications.

The *synchronized* keyword

The problem with the *run* method in the previous example, is that it can be interrupted at a critical moment. If you use the *synchronized* keyword when defining a method only one thread at a time will be allowed in that method. The *run* method can be amended to call a *synchronized* method:

```
public void run( ) {
    while (true)
        updateValue( );
}

public synchronized void updateValue( ) {
    myValue = 0;
    myValue++;
    if (value == 0 )System.out.println("value is " + myValue);
}
```

This application never displays the message *value is 0*, since once the *updateValue* method has been called it cannot be interrupted.

An alternative way of using *synchronized* allows you to ensure than only a part of the method cannot be interrupted:

```
public void updateValue( ) {
    myValue = 0;
    synchronized(this) {
        myValue++;
        if (myValue == 0 )System.out.println("value is " + myValue);
    }
}
```

The *synchronized* keyword is followed by the object that you want to prevent being changed by another thread, Using *this* specifies the instance itself and in this case has the same effect as applying synchronized to the whole method.

It is a good idea to keep to a minimum the size of methods which are synchronized. If your threads are only reading variables then there will be no problem, but if they are changing values you need to use *synchronized* to avoid introducing subtle bugs into your application.

Every Java class is thread safe, that is will not cause problems however many threads you use. However it is essential to be aware of possible problems when using code that you have written.

Using *Runnable*

The threads we have created have been subclasses of *java.lang.Thread* however you may wish to subclass another class. You can do this by using the *Runnable* keyword:

```
public class MyRunnableClass extends SomeClass implements Runnable{
    ....
}
```

The keyword *Runnable* indicates that an instance of this class is to be run as a separate thread. One problem is that the *Runnable* interface only implements the *run* method and not the *start, stop, suspend* and *resume* methods. To get around this problem, create an instance of the *Runnable* class:

```
MyRunnableClass myInstance = new MyRunnableClass( );
```

Next, use *new* to create an instance of the *Thread* class passing the instance of the *Runnable* class to it:

```
Thread myThread = new Thread(myInstance);
```

You can start the thread running by using the *start* method:

```
myThread.start( );
```

As usual, this calls the *run* method which contains the body of the code for the thread.

Thread priorities

In all the applications that we have looked at so far all the threads have had the same priority, that is, they are regarded as being equally important. The scheduler in most operating systems, including Windows 95, uses a priority scheduling scheme to decide which thread to run next. When the scheduler has to choose which of the threads in the ready state to run next, it will always choose the thread with the highest priority. A thread will never run while there is a thread with a higher priority ready to run. If there is more than one thread with the highest priority, the scheduler will run each of them in turn, choosing the one which has been waiting longest to run.

If we revisit the application where we have two threads, the priority is not specified, therefore the default priority is used:

- NORM_PRIORITY is the default priority assigned to a thread = 5.
- MAX_PRIORITY is the maximum thread priority = 10.
- MIN_PRIORITY is the minimum thread priority = 1.

The applications looks like this:

```
public class MultiThreads extends Thread {
    public static void main(String args[ ]) {
        MultiThreads myT1 = new MultiThreads( );
        myT1.start( );
        MultiThreads myT2 = new MultiThreads( );
        myT2.start(  );
    }

    public void run( ) {
        while (true) {
            System.out.println("Thread" +Thread.currentThread().getName
            }
        }
    }
}
```

This application prints:

```
Thread-1
Thread-1
Thread-1
Thread-2
Thread-2
....
```

If you want a thread to pause itself and to allow the scheduler to run another thread you can use the *yield* method:

```
while (true) {
    System.out.println("Thread "+Thread.currentThread( ).getName
        Thread.yield( );
    }
```

This will print:

```
Thread-1
Thread-2
Thread-1
....
```

You can find out the priority of a thread using the *getPriority* method:

```
myT1Priority = getPriority(myT1);
```

You can set the priority using the *setPriority* method:

```
myT1.setPriority(MAX_PRIORITY);
```

Even if a high priority task uses the *yield* method, a task with a lower priority will never run.

This may sound strange, but usually a thread will have changing priorities throughout its lifetime, however it does require careful management to avoid indefinite postponement. This occurs when a thread which is ready to run is prevented from doing so by a higher priority thread, just as that thread is about to finish another high priority thread starts. If this happens repeatedly, the lower priority thread is continually prevented from running and is said to be indefinitely postponed.

Animation

Now that we have covered the difficult area of multithreading, you have the background to write animations. Drawing basic shapes and images is straightforward in Java, it is also easy to create simple animation, although the main problem you are likely to encounter is that the animation is not very smooth, since programs written in Java will run a lot slower than similar programs written in languages such as Visual C++ or Delphi. Fortunately Java does support a technique called double buffering which makes the animation appear smoother.

The bouncing ball applet

It may seem at this stage that multithreading is only used when you have a complicated applet which is attempting to do more than one thing at a time, but in fact you need to use multithreading to create even simple animations. This is not apparent if you read the tutorial information on the Borland Web pages, and is a real source of problems, particularly since one of the most common uses of Java is to create animations.

The first animation applet we are going to look at, is of a ball which bounces around the edges of the screen. The ball starts off at a random position on the screen and moves initially in a random direction. When it reaches an edge it bounces back. The direction of travel is shown in fig. 7.2

Initially we are going to try and write this applet without using threaded code. The attempt is not successful, but it is worthwhile looking at it, since it does show how a reasonable, sensible approach to the problem is not viable. It also illustrates how central the ideas of using threaded code are to this key application area.

The ball is drawn at successive locations in the *paint* method, using the *setColor* method to change the colour of the ball to green and the *fillOval* method which draws the ball.

```
g.setColor(Color.green);
g.fillOval((int)x,(int)y,20,20);
```

The position of the ball is specified by the first two parameters in the *fillOval* method, these parameters are integers. In this example, however, x and y are defined as double quantities and so must be explicitly cast as integers by placing *(int)* before each of them.

The limits of the area in which the ball bounces is given by 0 to *xLimit* for the *x* values and 0 to *yLimit* for the *y* values.

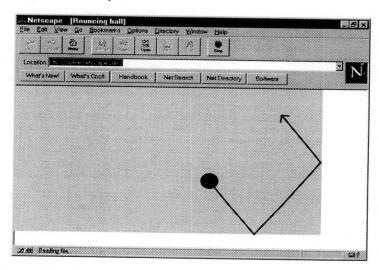

Fig. 7.2 *The bouncing ball applet showing the direction of bounce.*

The change in *x* and *y* every time the ball is drawn is given by *xChange* and *yChange*. These are assigned randomly using a random number generating method as shown below:

```
xChange = Math.random( );
yChange = Math.random( );
```

The method *Math.random* produces a double length floating point value.

The starting value of the ball is also created randomly as shown below. Values between 0 and the limit values are created using the code shown below.

```
x = Math.random( )* xLimit);
y = Math.random( )* yLimit);
```

The variable declaration and initialisation parts of the applet now look like this:

```
import java.awt. *;
public class Bounce extends java.applet.Applet {

double x, y, xChange, yChange;
double xLimit = 300;
double yLimit = 300;

public void init( ) {
    setBackground(Color.white);
    xChange = Math.random( );
    yChange = Math.random( );
```

```
    x = Math.random( )* xLimit);
    y = Math.random( )* yLimit);
    }
}
```

At this point it would seem that all that is needed to achieve a moving ball is to calculate successive new positions for the ball, to erase the previous image and to draw the new one, however it is not as simple as that. The code shown below is an endless loop that does this and could be used to make up the *start* method:

```
public void start( ) {
    while (true) {
        x += xChange;
        y += yChange;
        if ((x >= xLimit) | (x <= 0)) xChange = -xChange;
        if ((y >= yLimit) | (y <= 0)) yChange = -yChange;
        repaint( );
        }
    }
}
```

- Lines 3 and 4 of the *start* method add *xChange* and *yChange* to the old values of *x* and *y* and so calculate a new position.
- Lines 5 and 6 deal with the situation when one of the boundaries is reached, and change the sign of the value which is added to *x* or *y* to calculate the next position.
- Line 7 uses the *repaint* method. This calls the *update* method which erases the screen and then calls the *paint* method. The paint method draws the green ball using the *fillOval* method, that is:

```
g.setColor(Color.green);
g.fillOval((int)x,(int)y,20,20);
```

It would seem at this stage that we have a completed applet if the code for calculating the new position of the ball is placed in the *init* method, however if you do try and run this applet you will find that no ball is displayed. This is because the endless loop is taking up so much system time that there is no time available for anything else to run, including the *paint* method which actually causes the ball to be displayed. In order to solve this problem you need to use threaded code.

Using Threads

If a Java applet runs and executes a single series of instructions from initialisation to the end it is said to have one thread of control, but if you are writing an animation program you need to have multiple threads of control within the program. In this example, if the calculating of the new *x* and *y* positions was one thread and the drawing of the ball was another thread then the program would be able to carry out both operations, rather than spending all of its time on performing the calculations. Generally, when you have an applet in which there is one operation which continues for a long time, such as an animation or a long calculation, then it is best to place it within a separate thread from the rest of the applet.

Java allows you to write multithreaded applets. There are several changes that you need to make to the bouncing ball program to make it work:

- Add the words implements *Runnable* to the signature of the class of your applet.
- Create an instance variable for the applets thread.
- Create and start the thread in the *start* method.
- Put the code which calculates the new ball position into a new method called *run*.
- Add the *stop* method which stops the applet running when you leave the page.

The first two lines of the applet look like this:

```
import java.awt.*;
public class Bounce extends java.applet.Applet implements Runnable {
```

The instance variable declaration is as follows:

```
Thread ball;
```

This defines *ball* as being of a class called *Thread* which is defined in *java.lang*. The *start* method looks like this:

```
public void start( ) {
    if (ball == null); {
        ball = new Thread(this);
        ball.start( );
        }
    }
```

This code creates (or spawns in UNIX jargon) a new thread.
The code which calculates the new positions goes into the *run* method:

```
public void run( ) {
    while (true) {
        x += xChange;
        y += yChange;
        if ((x >= xLimit) | (x <= 0)) xChange = -xChange;
        if ((y >= yLimit) | (y <= 0)) yChange = -yChange;
        repaint( );
        try { Thread.sleep(10); }
        catch (InterruptedException e) { }
        }
    }
```

Any code which is in the *run* method runs in its own thread. Note that after the call to the *repaint* method there are two lines which have the effect of pausing for 10 milliseconds. The details of how to use *try* and *catch* are covered later.

The *stop* method stops the thread when you leave the page and sets the ball variable to null. This allows the applet to be removed from memory if you leave the page. The thread is started again when you return to the page, by the *start* method which checks the value of *ball*. The *stop* method looks like this:

```
public void stop( ) {
    if (ball != null) {
        ball.stop( );
        ball = null;
        }
    }
```

This is the completed applet:

```
import java.awt.*;
public class Bounce extends java.applet.Applet implements Runnable {

double x, y, xChange, yChange;
double xLimit = 300;
double yLimit = 300;
Thread ball;

public void init( ) {
    setBackground(Color.white);
    xChange = Math.random( );
    yChange = Math.random( );
    x = Math.random( )* xLimit;
    y = Math.random( )* yLimit;
    }

public void start( ) {
    if (ball == null); {
        ball = new Thread(this);
        ball.start( );
        }
    }
public void stop( ) {
    if (ball != null) {
        ball.stop( );
        ball = null;
        }
    }

public void run( ) {
```

```
while (true) {
    x += xChange;
    y += yChange;
    if ((x >= xLimit) | (x <= 0)) xChange = -xChange;
    if ((y >= yLimit) | (y <= 0)) yChange = -yChange;
    repaint( );
    try { Thread.sleep(1); }
    catch (InterruptedException e) { }
    }
}

public void paint(Graphics g) {
    g.setColor(Color.green);
    g.fillOval((int)x,(int)y,20,20);
    }
}
```

Reducing flicker

There is still one annoying problem with this animation and the slower your computer, the worse the problem. The bouncing ball flickers as it moves, this is because the entire screen is redrawn every time that the ball is drawn. When you call the *repaint* method this calls the *update* method which clears the screen, which in turn calls the *paint* method. There are two solutions to the problem.

- Override the standard *update* method by writing your own and not clearing the screen. In the bouncing ball applet this is not appropriate since you do need to clear the previous image of the ball to create the impression of movement. In the following example, where the image does not need to be erased every time a new image is drawn, this technique is very effective.
- Use double buffering. This involves creating the image in an area of memory and when the image is complete, transferring it to the screen. This is particularly useful if the creation of the screen requires a lot of time-consuming calculations.

Overriding methods

In chapter 4 we looked at overriding the constructor methods which are called when an object is created. In the same way you can override any other method, you do this by creating a new method which has the same name as the method you wish to override in the superclass. In the next section you will see the *update* method being overridden to improve the performance of animation in an applet. How does Java know which method to use if there is more than one which have the same name? If you use method overloading Java differentiates between the methods because they have different parameter lists. In method overriding the methods may have the same name and different parameters.

When a method is referred to, Java looks for a method for the class of the current object. If it finds one, it uses it. If it does not find a method it looks at the superclass, and so on up the class hierarchy until it finds a match.

The best way to appreciate how this works is to look at an example of how it is used.

Overriding *update*

Most of us have played the Windows version of solitaire, where the cards fly across the screen at the end of the game. Each suit of cards is left in four piles at the top of the screen if you have won. Each card in turn then flies across in a random direction at a random speed leaving a trail behind it showing the path that it has followed.

This applet reproduces the flying cards as shown in fig. 7.3, except that only one pile of cards is used.

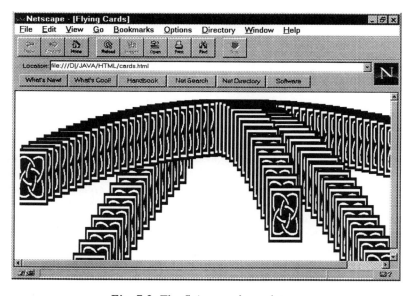

Fig. 7.3 The flying cards applet.

In this applet previous images are not erased when a new one is drawn. This is achieved by overriding the *update* method by including your own. Java does not need to look up through the class hierarchy at the superclasses of the current class where the default *update* method is found, since it finds an *update* method within this class. In this case all that *update* does is to call *paint* as shown below:

```
public void update(Graphics g) {
    paint(g);
}
```

Apart from adding this method the applet has the same structure as the bouncing example. The completed program is shown below.

```
import java.awt.*;
public class Cards extends java.applet.Applet implements Runnable {
    double x, y, xVelocity, yAcceleration, xStart;
    double xLimit = 800;
    double yLimit = 300;
    int time;
    Thread flying;
    Image img;

    public void init( ) {
        setBackground(Color.white);
        img = getImage(getCodeBase( ),"card.gif");
    }
    public void start( ) {
        if (flying == null); {
            flying = new Thread(this);
            flying.start( );
        }
    }
    public void stop( ) {
        if (flying != null) {
            flying.stop( );
            flying = null;
        }
    }

    public void run( ) {
        xStart = xlimit/2;
        while (true) {
            x=0;
            y=0;
            time = 0;
// x velocity is a random value between -25 and +25
            xVelocity = (Math.random( ) - 0.5) * 50.0;
            yAcceleration = Math.random( );
            while (((x >= 0) && (x <= xLimit)) &&
                    ((y >= 0) && (y <= yLimit))) {
// x position is velocity * time
                x = xStart + xVelocity * (double)time;
// y position is proportional to acceleration * time squared
                y = yAcceleration * (double)time * (double)time;
                time ++;
                repaint( );
```

```
            try { Thread.sleep(100);}
            catch (InterruptedException e) {}
            }
        }
    }
    public void update(Graphics g) {
        paint(g);
    }
    public void paint(Graphics g) {
        g.drawImage(img,(int)x,(int)y, 70, 120, this);
    }
}
```

There are some useful things to notice in this applet, The card is a gif file called *card.gif*. This is in the same location as the HTML file and the *getCodeBase* method is used to specify this in the *init* method as shown below:

$$img = getImage(getCodeBase(\ ),"card.gif");$$

If you want to try this example for yourself, you can use any gif file, which looks as if it might represent the back of a playing card.

The gif file is opened once only, when the applet is initialised, it is drawn repeatedly in the *paint* method. Since *paint* is used every time an object is drawn on the screen it is best to keep it as simple as possible, so methods such as *setBackground* should be called in another method, usually *init* is the best place.

When carrying out calculations in Java using a variety of different classes it is best to explicitly cast the variables, for example:

$$x = xStart + xVelocity * (double)time;$$

x is defined as double length floating point, while *time* is an integer, putting *(double)* in front of *time* casts it explicitly as double.

The card has a constant velocity in the x direction, but is accelerated in the y direction, so its velocity increases. The initial values of *xVelocity* and *yAcceleration* are chosen randomly. The positions of the card are calculated by the general equations of motion, but if you are not interested in the maths used to calculate the positions of the card do not worry about it, you do not need to be a good mathematician to be a good programmer. The key feature of this applet is the overriding of the *update* method by supplying your own.

Using double buffering

Double buffering is a classic way of reducing flicker of animations. Rather than drawing your animation directly onto the screen you draw onto another surface and when the image is completed you transfer it directly to the screen. Double buffering is very effective in practice, mainly because it removes the pauses which occur when drawing each part of the screen, perhaps while calculations are carried out. It is only when all the calculations and the off screen drawing are complete that the next frame in the animation is displayed.

The running applet shown in fig. 7.4 shows a pendulum swinging from side to side and back again. We are going to write the applet first without double buffering and then modify it to use double buffering. You will see a great improvement in the performance of the applet. If double buffering is not used, the flicker is awful even with a fast Pentium processor and high performance graphics card!

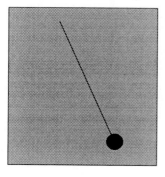

Fig. 7.4 *The pendulum applet.*

This applet not only give you the opportunity to try double buffering, but also brings out a few of the practical problems of creating even a simple animation like this. To perform any animation often requires some knowledge of geometry - as you will see in this example. If you are not too interested in this aspect you can omit it and concentrate on the techniques for reducing flicker.

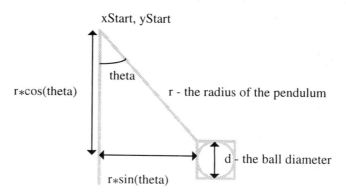

Fig. 7.5 *Calculating the position of the swinging pendulum.*

The new positions of the swinging ball are calculated as it moves. One important point to notice is that when a circle is drawn with the *fillOval* method, it is given four parameters, the first two fixing its position. The co-ordinates that you specify give the position of the top left corner of a square enclosing the circle as shown in fig. 7.5, not the position of the centre. The position of the top left corner in the horizontal, *x* direction is given by *r * sin(theta)*, where *r* is the radius of the pendulum, and *theta* is the current angle of swing. The position of the centre of the ball is given by:

$$x = r * sin(theta) + b$$

Where *b* is the radius of the ball. Similarly the vertical *y* position of the centre of the ball is given by:

$$y = r * cos(theta) + b$$

Two methods *Math.cos* and *Math.sin* are used in these calculations.

One final complication is that these methods only deal with angles expressed in radians not degrees. If your maths is rusty $360° = 2\pi$ radians.

The organisation of the applet is similar to the bouncing ball applet. The *run* method, where the new position of the ball is calculated, is shown below:

```
public void run( ) {
    while (true) {
        x = xStart + (int)(r * Math.sin(theta));
        y = yStart + (int)(r * Math.cos(theta));
        if ((theta >= thetaMax) | (theta <= thetaMin)) change = -change;
        theta += change;
        repaint( );
        try { Thread.sleep(10); }
        catch (InterruptedException e) { }
        }
    }
```

x and *y* are the position of the centre of the pendulum. The angle of the pendulum relative to the vertical is varied by change every time the pendulum is drawn. When the new pendulum angle is calculated to be greater than or equal to the maximum permitted value, *thetaMax,* the variable *change* retains the same magnitude, but becomes a negative value. When this is added to *theta*, it makes *theta* start to decrease. When *theta* becomes smaller than or equal to the minimum permitted value of *theta, thetaMin,* the variable *change* is changed from a negative to a positive value and *theta* will start to increase again. The *repaint* method is called to redraw the pendulum and a *try* and *catch* clause ensure that the pendulum is drawn every 10 milliseconds.

The completed applet is shown below:

```
import java.awt.*;   //Pendulum WITHOUT double buffering
public class pendulum extends java.applet.Applet implements Runnable {
//The position of the centre of the swinging pendulum
    int x, y;
//The extremes of the pendulum swing in radians
    double thetaMax = (double)0.35, thetaMin = (double)-0.35;
//The initial position of the pendulum
    double theta = (double)0,
//The change in position of the pendulum every time it is drawn
    change = (double)0.01;
//The point the pendulum swings about
    int xStart = 150, yStart = 20;
//The radius of the pendulum
```

```
    double r = (double)200;
//The diameter of the ball
    int d = 20;
    Thread ball;

public void init( ) {
setBackground(Color.white);
}

public void start( ) {
    if (ball == null); {
        ball = new Thread(this);
        ball.start( );
        }
    }
public void stop( ) {
    if (ball != null) {
        ball.stop( );
        ball = null;
        }
    }

public void run( ) {
    while (true) {
        x = xStart + (int)(r * Math.sin(theta));
        y = yStart + (int)(r * Math.cos(theta));
        if ((theta >= thetaMax) | (theta <= thetaMin)) change = -change;
        theta += change;
        repaint( );
        try { Thread.sleep(10); }
        catch (InterruptedException e) { }
        }
    }

public void paint(Graphics g) {
    g.setColor(Color.blue);
    g.drawLine(xStart, yStart, x, y);
    g.setColor(Color.red);
//if the centre of the circle is at x, y the top left corner is at  x-d/2, y-d/2
    g.fillOval(x-d/2,y-d/2, d, d);
    }
}
```

This applet works successfully, but it does flicker a lot. The flicker can be reduced by using double buffering, where the image to be shown is created in the background and when it is completed it is drawn on the screen.

The first stage is to create an instance of the *Image* class to draw the image on and an instance of the *Graphics* class that allows all the usual drawing methods to be used on it:

```
Image backgroundImage;
Graphics backgroundGraphics;
```

Next these instances have to be initialised in the *init* method:

```
public void init( ) {
    setBackground(Color.white);
    backgroundImage = createImage(this.size( ).width, this.size( ).height);
    backgroundGraphics = backgroundImage.getGraphics( );
}
```

The *createImage* method creates an instance of the *Image* class which is used to provide a new graphics context. The size of the image object is not known until run time - so *this.size( ).width* and *this.size( ).height* have been used to provide this at run time.

A new *update* method has been provided to override the default *update* method and to prevent the screen being cleared every time *paint* is called:

```
public void update(Graphics g) {
    paint(g);
}
```

Finally the *paint* method has been changed. The previous image of the pendulum is overwritten, before drawing the new image, the line and circle of the pendulum are drawn again in white, the colour of the background, rather than erasing the whole image for speed. Note that at the end of *paint*, the position of the pendulum is saved in the variables *oldX* and *oldY*. It is only when the pendulum has been drawn in the new position that the image is displayed on the screen by the line:

```
g.drawImage(backgroundImage, 0, 0, this);
```

The whole of the *paint* method used is shown below:

```
public void paint(Graphics g) {
//erase then old image
    backgroundGraphics.setColor(Color.white);
    backgroundGraphics.drawLine(xStart, yStart, oldX, oldY);
    backgroundGraphics.fillOval(oldx-d/2, oldy-d/2, d, d);
//draw the new image
    backgroundGraphics.setColor(Color.blue);
    backgroundGraphics.drawLine(xStart, yStart, x, y);
    backgroundGraphics.setColor(Color.red);
    backgroundGraphics.fillOval(x-d/2,y-d/2,d,d);
//now display the image
    g.drawImage(backgroundImage,0,0,this);
    oldX = x;
    oldY = y;
```

```
        }
    }
```

One of the most common uses of Java is to produce animation. Java does have an excellent syntax and range of tools for creating multithreaded applications and applets and for creating basic shapes and importing images. It is disappointing though, that there tends to be a lot of flicker with Java animations. This is mainly because Java is interpreted by the browser and therefore runs a lot slower than if a program written in a comparable language was run on the same computer. This problem is being addressed for future releases of Java and is certain to improve. Processors are becoming faster and graphics cards are becoming better and cheaper, which will also be a great benefit. There is a significant improvement running an animated Java applet on a fast Pentium based computer compared to a DX2 or DX4 based computer.

8

Handling Exceptions

Introduction

We all like to think that our applications do not have errors in them, but in reality every piece of software that we use has bugs. Some are simply errors in the logic of the program, others are caused by unexpected input from the user. Sometimes problems occur because of the physical limitations of the computer, such as running out of memory. If we could guarantee that situations like this would never happen it would make programming much easier, but this is unfortunately not the case.

Java provides some useful tools for managing unexpected situations which occur in applications.

In this chapter you will learn how to:

- Use exceptions.
- Declare that exceptions may occur in a class.
- Use *try* and *catch* to deal with exceptions.

What are exceptions?

In Java, exceptions occur when some error condition arises, such as running out of memory or a reference to a class which does not exist.

Java exceptions

A Java exception is an instance of the *Throwable* class, which is a subclass of the java.lang package.

The class hierarchy for the *Throwable* class is shown in fig 8.1

The *Throwable* class has two sub classes *Exception* and *Error*. The distinction between errors and exceptions is not a hard and fast one. Exceptions are exceptional conditions that the programmer may need to take some action to deal with, such as referring to a non-existent method. Errors tend to be caused by problems with the environment which the applet is working within, that is in the virtual machine that the applet runs on, such as running out of memory.

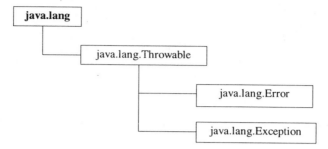

Fig. 8.1 The class hierarchy for the Throwable class.

The *java.lang.Exception* class

The *java.lang.Exception* class has 9 sub classes as shown in fig 8.2

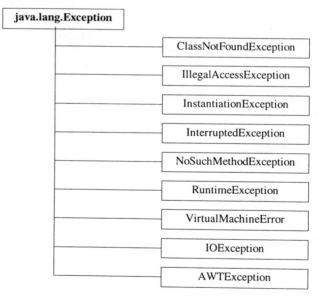

Fig. 8.2 The class hierarchy for the Exception class.

When you are planning a way of dealing with exceptions in your applets you need to consider which exceptions will occur in each method. You do this by using the *throws* clause, for example you can declare a method as:

public void myMethod( ) {

If this method could produce the *InterruptedException* exception you would specify this by changing the declaration to:

> *public void myMethod( ) throws InterruptedException {*

This sounds straightforward until you realise that the *RunTimeException*, the *VirtualMachineError*, the *IOException* and the *AWTException* class each have sub classes, and that these could occur in any method, for example the errors in the *VirtualMachineErrors* class include *OutOfMemory*, *StackOverFlowError* and *UnknownError*. Fortunately, instances of the *RunTimeException* class (and the *Error* class) do not have to be listed and are included implicitly for you. These instances usually occur due to situations beyond the control of the programmer and are related to the virtual running environment.

Trying and catching

So far, we have looked at a way of flagging that a particular exception may occur in a method. We have not looked at how to handle it. If you do list an exception in the *throws* clause you are not required by Java to take any further action. You can view this clause simply as a flag to yourself or other software developers that this exception can occur. The caller of this method can then take some action to deal with the exception. It is effectively a way of passing the problem down the line, and is rather bad practice. It is best to sort out problems as soon as they occur. If the caller does not take any action either to deal with the exception, they may be caught higher in the system, if they are not they will eventually be caught by the environment and an error message produced.

If you do decide to deal with exceptions where they occur you can omit the throw clause and use the *try* and *catch* clauses instead, for example:

```
try {
    myNewMethod( );
}
catch (InterruptedException) {
    ...
}
}
```

When the exception occurs within the *try* clause, control is passed to the appropriate *catch* clause. The action you want to take to deal with the exception goes in between the { } brackets. If you are finding this confusing try the example program below. It is an application rather than an applet, since it is easier to display simple text using a stand alone application.

```
class Hello {
public static void main (String args[ ]) {
    int c;
    int a[ ] = new int[2];
    try {
```

```
            for (c=0; c<10; c++) {
                a[c] = c;
                System.out.println("Array element " + c + " is legal");
                }
            }
        catch(ArrayIndexOutOfBoundsException e) {
        System.out.println("Whoops");
            }
        }
    }
```

This application defines an array of two elements. When it attempts to write to element *a[2]* (the third element) the *ArrayIndexOutOfBoundsException* occurs. The application prints out the following test before ending:

```
    Array element 0 is legal
    Array element 1 is legal
    Whoops
```

You are not limited to having one *catch* clause, you can have a list of them as shown below:

```
    try {
        myNewMethod( ) {
        ...
        }
    catch (ArithmeticException); {

        ....
        }
    catch (IndexOutOfBoundsException); {
        ...
        }
    catch (SecurityException); {
        ...
    }
```

Control will be transferred to the appropriate *catch* clause to deal with the exception. One useful way of using these lists of *catch* clauses is if you wish to deal with a specific exception in a particular way and all the other members of the same superclass in a different way. You do not need to list all the sub classes, for example:

```
    try {
        myNewMethod( ) {
        ...
        }
    catch (IndexOutOfBoundsException); {
        ...
        }
```

```
catch (RuntimeException) {
    ...
}
catch (Throwable) {
    ...
}
```

The *IndexOutOfBounds* class is a sub class of the *RuntimeException* class, so all the other *RuntimeExceptions* classes will be caught in the second *catch* statement. The third *catch* clause will *catch* any remaining exceptions since all are members of the *Throwable* class.

Throwing and catching

We have looked at using the *throw* clause to indicate that an exception may occur in a method and the *try* and *catch* clauses to deal with exceptions when they occur. You can use *throw* and also *try* and *catch* in the same method. This allows you to handle the exception yourself, but still indicates to the caller that the exception has occurred. The *try* and *catch* clauses are the same as before, except that you need to explicitly throw the exception after handling it, for example:

```
catch(ArrayIndexOutOfBoundsException e) {
    ....
    throw e;
}
```

Using *finally*

The *finally* clause is an important addition to Java which is not found in C++. When an exception occurs you can trap it, but sometimes there is something that you always want your application or applet to do regardless of what has happened. Perhaps you want to make sure that all your files are closed, and all system resources are freed. The *finally* clause lets you do this for example:

```
finally {
    closeFiles( );
    freeSystemResources( );
}
```

The *finally* clause is always the last clause to be completed whether an exception or anything else happens in either your application or applet.

9

The java.awt Package

Introduction

All of the applications that we use every day, such as browsers, word processors and spreadsheets, are made up of standard components, including buttons, lists and edit boxes. The visual programming languages such as Delphi and Visual Basic allow you to develop professional standard user interfaces for your applications easily. Java has access to a set of standard components through the Abstract Windowing Toolkit or AWT. The toolkit is in the package *java.awt*. If you are familiar with visual programming you will find many of the concepts such as event driven programming and the use of components to build graphical user interfaces more straightforward.

In this chapter you will learn about:

- Event driven programming.
- The key components of the *java.awt* package.
- How to control the layout of components using the layout managers.

This chapter looks at a sample of the classes in the AWT, a full list and class hierarchy are given in Appendices A and B.

Event driven programming

Programs written for a UNIX or DOS environment present you with a prompt to input information and will not proceed until you have responded to that prompt. In contrast when you are using an application in a Windows environment you are presented with a screen which is a collection of text boxes, buttons, images, lists and menus and you can then decide what to do. These constituent parts of the screen are called components. Programs of this type, written in a Windows visual programming language or Java, are said to be event driven. You decide what action to take such as pressing a button, entering text in a text box, or choosing an item from a list. The order in which you do these things is usually not important. Every time you take some action, an event occurs and the program needs to have an event handler that will deal with that event. If, for example, you click a button, there needs to be some code which will be run when the button click event occurs. This is the button click event handler. Some components such as buttons support more than one event, such as click and double click. Java provides both a set of standard components and also an environment for supporting the writing of event driven software as we shall see in this chapter.

What the AWT does

The AWT provides you with:

- A set of standard components such as buttons, text boxes and list boxes.
- A set of container components. The standard components mentioned are drawn onto the container components.
- An environment for creating event handlers for the components.

Initially we are going to look at some of the standard components. If you are used to a visual programming environment these will be familiar to you. What will seem different though is the way in which the position of these components in the window is controlled. This is covered later in the chapter, when we have seen some components and can look at how to control their position.

The *Button* component

One of the most common components is the *Button*. The example below in the file *MyButton.java* draws three buttons as shown in fig. 9.1.

The code sets the default font to 40 point Arial. This is done in subsequent examples in this chapter, but is not shown.

The *init* function is executed when the program is run.

```
import java.awt.*;
public class MyButton extends java.applet.Applet {

public void init( ) {
    Font theFont = new Font("Arial",Font.PLAIN,40);
    setFont (theFont);
    add(new Button("OK"));
    add(new Button("Cancel"));
    add(new Button("Options"));
    add(new Button("Help"));
    }
}
```

Note that the line:

```
    add(new Button("OK"));
```

is a shorthand way of writing:

```
Button myNewButton = new Button("OK");
add(myNewButton);
```

If you want a button without any label, you can use the statement:

```
add(new Button( ));
```

The HTML file, *MyButton.html*, is shown below and gives a title and a reference to the *MyButton* class which is defined in the file *MyButton.java*.

```
<HTML>
<HEAD>
<TITLE> The Button component </TITLE>
</HEAD>
<BODY>
<APPLET CODE = "MyButton.class" width=600 height=300>
</APPLET>
</BODY>
</HTML>
```

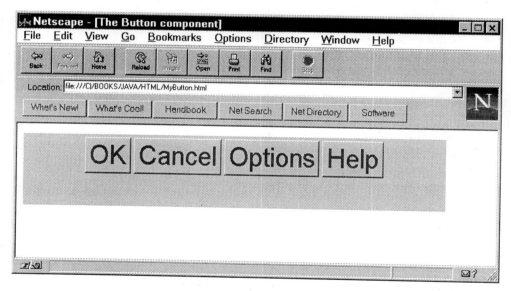

Fig. 9.1 *The Button component.*

The buttons are aligned left to right in the centre of the shaded area in the order in which they are specified. The positioning is a feature of the container that the component is drawn on. In this case the default is used. This important aspect is looked at later in this chapter.

The most useful methods for the button component are shown in table 9.1.

Table 9.1 *The methods of the Button component.*

Method	Description
getLabel( )	Returns the label on the button.
setLabel(String)	Changes the label of the button to the new string.

The *Label* component

The *Label* component is used to display a single line of read only text.

> *add(new) Label("first label"));*
> *add(new) Label("second label"));*
> *add(new) Label("third label"));*

first label   second label   third label   *Fig. 9.2* *The Label component.*

If you want to specify the alignment of the labels you can add an additional parameter after the text as shown below:

> *add(new) Label("centred label", label.CENTER));*

centred label   *Fig. 9.3* *The Label component.*

There are limitations however, if more than one label is displayed on the same line, they are simply placed in the order in which they are specified. The alignment parameter has no effect.

The most useful methods for the *Label* component are:

Table 9.2 *The methods of the Label component.*

Method	Description
getAlignment( )	Returns the alignment of the label. 0=left, 1=centre, 2=right.
getText( )	Returns the text on the label.
setAlignment(int)	Sets the labels alignment.
setText(String)	Changes the text in the label.

The *Scrollbar* component

The *Scrollbar* component is used to allow you to carry out a range of functions, for example if a list is displayed and it is too large to fit into the available space, a scrollbar allows you to move through the list, you can write code to move in proportion to the degree of movement on the scrollbar. The position of the box on the slider indicates the *value* property of the slider between a user defined minimum and maximum. You can move the box either by clicking on the arrows at either end of the scrollbar or by dragging the box as shown in fig. 9.4.

Arrows

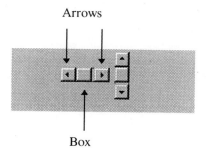

Fig. 9.4   The Scrollbar component.

Box

Scrollbars are so useful that they have been built into several other components, for example, the *List* and *TextArea* components, which are covered later in this chapter.

Table 9.3 *The methods of the Scrollbar component.*

Method	Description
getMaximum( )	Gets the maximum value of the scrollbar.
getMinimum( )	Gets the minimum value.
getOrientation( )	Returns the orientation of the scrollbar (either horizontal or vertical.
getValue( )	Gets the current value of the scrollbar.
getValues(int,int,int,int)	Gets the value, size, minimum and maximum values of the scrollbar.
setValue(int)	Sets the current value of the Scrollbar.
setValues(int,int,int,int)	Sets the value, size, minimum and maximum values of the scrollbar.

Scrollbars can be either vertical or horizontal. The default is vertical. To create scrollbars you can use the following code:

```
add(new Scrollbars( ));
add(new Scrollbar(Scrollbar.HORIZONTAL);
```

There is no need to specify that the first scrollbar is vertical with the *Scrollbar.VERTICAL* constant. The two scrollbars created are shown in fig. 9.4.

In addition to specifying the orientation of the scrollbar there are four other parameters:

- The initial value of the scrollbar which must be between the minimum and maximum values.
- The length of a horizontal scrollbar, or the height of a vertical scrollbar.
- The minimum value of the scrollbar.
- The maximum value of the scrollbar.

The line of code:

>   *add(new Scrollbar(Scrollbar.HORIZONTAL,20,100,1,100);*

produces a horizontal scrollbar with an initial value of 20, a width of 100, a minimum value of 1 and a maximum value of 100. In early versions of Java there was a bug which meant that the scrollbar component did not always perform correctly.

The most useful methods for the scrollbar component are shown in table 9.3.

The *Checkbox* component

Checkbox components consist of some text and a box which can either be checked or not. Checkboxes are most useful when you need to choose whether you want an option or not. It is useful to be able to group checkboxes together, so that only one of the group can be selected.

The checkboxes produced by the following code are shown in fig. 9.5:

>   *add(new Checkbox("80486DX4");*
>   *add(new Checkbox("Pentium P120");*
>   *add(new Checkbox("Pentium P166", null, true);*

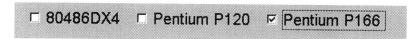

Fig. 9.5 *The Checkbox component.*

The first string parameter gives the text adjacent to the checkbox. The third parameter, found in the third checkbox, gives its state. The default state is *false* and so there is no need to specify it for the first two checkboxes. The *true* state is indicated by a tick in the box. The second parameter is set to null, this parameter is used when a number of checkboxes are to be grouped together and only one of the group can be set to *true*. This is the case when the options are mutually exclusive as shown in fig. 9.6. When checkboxes are used in this way they are called radio buttons and have a different appearance.

To create a set of radio buttons:

- Use the *CheckboxGroup* component,
- Add radio buttons to that group by using the second parameter in the add method.

An example is shown in this code:

>   *CheckboxGroup myGroup = new CheckboxGroup( );*
>
>   *add(new Checkbox("Female", myGroup, false));*
>   *add(new Checkbox("Male", myGroup, false));*

The radio buttons created are shown in fig. 9.6.

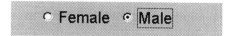

Fig. 9.6 *Radio buttons.*

When one of these radio buttons is selected, that is, set to *true*, the other is set to *false*, they cannot both be *true*.

The most commonly used methods of the checkbox component both when used as a radio button and as a standard checkbox component are listed below:

Table 9.4 *The methods of the Checkbox component.*

Method	Description
getCheckboxGroup( )	Returns the name of the checkbox group. This will be null if the checkbox is not a member of a group.
getLabel( )	Gets the text associated with the checkbox.
getState( )	Gets the state of the checkbox, either *true* or *false*.
setLabel(String)	Changes the checkbox text to the specified string.
setState(boolean)	Sets the checkbox to the specified state.

The *List* component

The *List* component provides a list of items for the user to select. If the size of the list is not big enough to include all the list items, a vertical scroll bar is automatically supplied as shown in fig. 9.7.

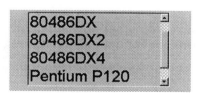

Fig. 9.7 *The List component.*

The code below creates the list box and puts the entries into it.

```
List myList = new List(4, false);
    myList.addItem("80486DX");
    myList.addItem("80486DX2");
    myList.addItem("80486DX4");
    myList.addItem("Pentium P120");
    myList.addItem("Pentium P166");
    add(mylist);
```

The list box is created in the same way as any other component using *new*. There are two parameters:

- The first parameter (a value of 4 in the example above) is the number of items that are visible at any one time.

- The second (*false* in this case) is set to *true* if you can select more than one entry.

To make the entries in the list, the *addItem* method is used. Finally to display the list the *add* method is used.

There are many methods for the list component, the most common are listed below:

Table 9.5 *The methods of the List component.*

Method	Description
getCheckboxGroup( )	Returns the name of the checkbox group. This will be null if the checkbox is not a member of a group.
getLabel( )	Gets the text associated with the checkbox.
getState( )	Gets the state of the checkbox, either true or false.
setLabel(String)	Changes the checkbox text to the specified string.
setState(boolean)	Sets the checkbox to the specified state.

The *TextField* component

This component is used to allow you to display and to edit text.

Table 9.6 *The methods of the TextField component.*

Method	Description
getText( )	Returns the text in the field.
SetText(String)	Changes the text in the component to the specified string.
getColumns( )	Gives the width of the text field.
select(int, int)	Selects the text between the specified positions. The start of the text is zero.
selectAll( )	selects all of the text.
isEditable( )	Returns a boolean which is *true* if the text is editable, and *false* if it is not.
setEditable(boolean)	If set to *true* the text is editable. If *false* it is not

```
add(new TextField("What is your favourite language? ",65));
add(new Label("Which do you prefer Windows 95 or UNIX?"));
add(new TextField(30));
```

Fig. 9.8 *The TextField component.*

The first parameter is a string which is displayed in the text field. The second is the size of the field. This allows the user to add additional text, for example to type a favourite programming language. An alternative way of prompting the user for input is to use a label and then a text field with a size, but no text specified.

The most important methods for this component are:

Entering passwords

The *TextField* component can be used for entering passwords. When a password is entered it is conventional to have one character displayed irrespective of which character is typed at the keyboard. A "*" is usually used. *The setEchoCharacter* method is used to specify the character which is displayed, for example;

```
TextField myText = new TextField(12);
myText.setEchoCharacter("*");
```

You can test to see if the component has a masking character by using the *echoCharIsset( )* method, which returns a boolean set to true if there is a masking character.

The *getEchoChar( )* method returns the masking character.

The *TextArea* component

The *TextArea* component is the last component that we are going to review in this chapter, it is used for displaying a large amount of text. You can specify the number of rows and columns. If all the text cannot be displayed in the available space, scroll bars are automatically added.

To create the *TextArea* component shown in fig. 9.9 use the following code:

```
String myString = "One of the key  advantages of Java is the\n" +
    ease with which you can develop\n" +
    develop interactive Web pages. At the\n" +
    moment there is no  other way if doing this\n" +
    One of the concerns especially with UNIX systems\n"+
    is that viruses will be distributed around the world\n" +
    by Java applets";
add(new TextArea(myString, 5, 40));
```

The first parameter is the string to be displayed, the second is the number of rows and the third the number of columns. If you want to create a blank text area, you can omit the first parameter, for example to create an empty area 10 rows by 55 columns:

```
TextArea(10, 55)
```

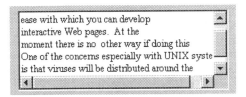

Fig. 9.9 *The TextArea component.*

The key methods for this component are:

Table 9.7 *The methods of the TextArea component.*

Method	Description
getColumns( )	Returns the number of columns.
getRows( )	Returns the number of rows.
insertText(String, int)	Inserts the given string at the specified position. The first position at the start of the text is zero.
replaceText(String, int, int)	Replaces the text between the specified positions with the given string.

Controlling layout

We have looked at some of the most common components, but so far we have not had any control over the position of these components on the Web page. If you are used to programming in a Windows environment with a visual programming language where you can simply drag and drop components, this section will seem to be tricky.

The screen can be divided into a number of panels. Each panel can have its own layout manager, which controls the appearance and position of the components which are placed on it.

There are 5 layout managers:

- *FlowLayout.*
- *GridLayout.*
- *GridBagLayout.*
- *BorderLayout.*
- *CardLayout.*

When you are designing your screen first choose the layout manager and then place the components on it. You cannot change the class of the panel that components are on.

The *FlowLayout* class

This is the default layout which is used if you do not explicitly say which layout you want. The example below produces figure 9.10:

```
import java.awt.*;
public class MyFlowLayout extends java.applet.Applet {
    public void init() {
        setLayout(new FlowLayout(FlowLayout.CENTER));
        add(new Button("FlowLayout"));
        add(new Button("class"));
        add(new Button("with"));
        add(new Button("CENTERED"));
        add (new Button("components"));
    }
}
```

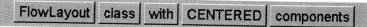

Fig. 9.10 *Centred components.*

As components are added they are displayed along a row with new components being added to the right of existing components. If a row is full, new components are moved onto a new line. The default alignment of components is centred, but you can change this to left by adding an additional parameter:

> setLayout(new FlowLayout(FlowLayout.LEFT));

Fig. 9.11 *Left aligned components.*

You can also specify *FlowLayout.CENTER* and *FlowLayout.RIGHT*.

There are two more parameters which allow you to control the spacing between the rows and columns, for example:

> SetLayout(new FlowLayout(FlowLayout.LEFT),20,10);

This instruction gives a horizontal gap of 20 between the rows and a vertical gap of 10 between the columns.

Most of the methods for the *FlowLayout* class are shared with the other layout classes and so these are covered in a separate section at the end of this chapter.

The *GridLayout* class

To display components in a grid layout use the *GridLayout* class.

```
SetLayout(new GridLayout(3,2));
    add(new Button("GridLayout"));
    add(new Button("class"));
    add(new Button("with"));
```

```
add(new Button("3 rows"));
add (new Button("2 columns"));
```

This code displays the five buttons in a grid 3 by 2 as shown in fig. 9.12.

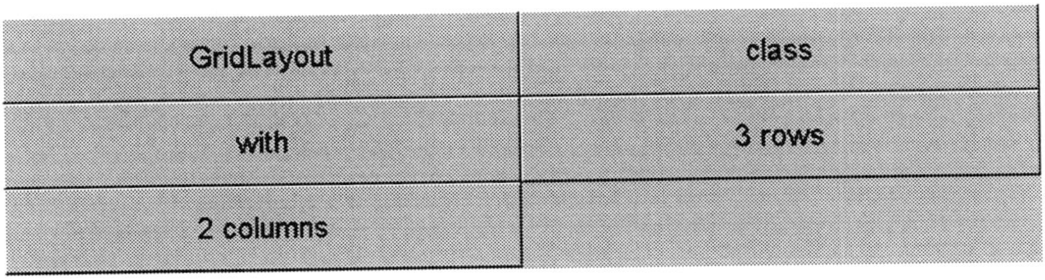

GridLayout	class
with	3 rows
2 columns	

Fig. 9.12 *The GridLayout class.*

There are a further two parameters which control the horizontal and vertical spacing, for example:

```
setLayout(new GridLayout(3,2,20,30));
```

The effect of this is shown in fig. 9.13.

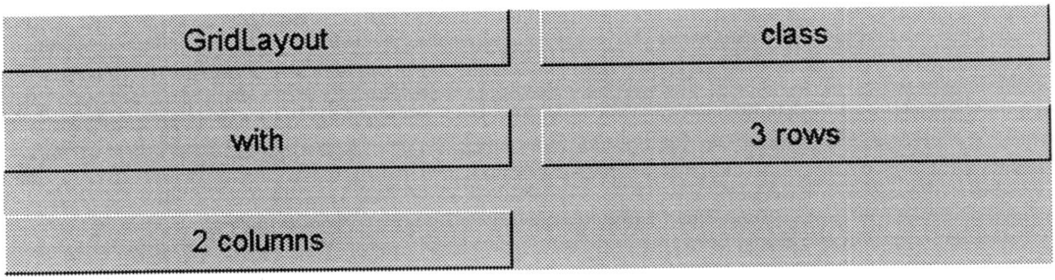

GridLayout	class
with	3 rows
2 columns	

Fig. 9.13 *The GridLayout class.*

The *GridBagLayout* class

The *GridBagLayout* class is the most recently introduced of the layout managers in Java, it is also the most flexible. This layout manager aligns components in a grid in which the grid cells can be of different sizes. Every *GridBagLayout* has an associated *GridBagConstraints* instance that determines how each component is laid out within the display area.

The most commonly used instance variables of the *GridBagConstraints* object are shown in table 9.8.

It is not easy to see how you would use all of these features, so here are a few examples to demonstrate the essential points.

Table 9.8 *Instance variables of the GridBagConstraints object.*

Instance Variable	Use
gridx, gridy	Specifies the cells position. the top left cell is 0,0.
gridwidth, gridheight	Specifies the number of cells in a row, and the number of columns.
fill	When the display area is larger than the components requested size, this variable is used to determine how to resize the component. *GridBagConstraint.HORIZONTAL* makes the component wide enough to fill the space. *GridBagConstraint.VERTICAL* makes the component tall enough. *GridbagConstraint.BOTH* makes the component big enough to entirely fill the display area.
anchor	When the component is smaller than the display area this variable is used to determine its positioning within the area. *GridbagConstraint.CENTER* puts the component in the centre of the area. The other possible values are: *NORTH, NORTHEAST, EAST, SOUTHEAST, SOUTHWEST, SOUTH, WEST* and *NORTHWEST*.
weightx, weighty	This variable specifies the relative weight of the components in a row. It is used to determine how to distribute space among the components and plays an important role when the grid is resized.

Whenever one of the instance variables is changed, the *setConstraints* method must be called. In this example, to simplify the procedure of creating new instances of the button object and using this method, a method called *newButton* has been written:

```
public void newButton( String name,
                  GridBagLayout gridbag,
                  GridBagConstraints c) {
    Button button = new Button(name);
    gridbag.setConstraints(button, c);
    add(button);
}
```

The layout manager is specified in the same way as for the other layout managers.

- The *weightx* variable is assigned the value 1.0 and then *NewButton* is called (which creates the button and calls the *setConstraints* method).
- The *weightx* value for the second button is then assigned the value 4.0, giving this button a size four times greater than the first button.
- The *gridwidth* variable is assigned to *GridBagConstraints.REMAINDER*, which indicates that the third button will fill all the remaining available space, and will therefore be the last button on the row.

```
public void init( ) {
    GridBagLayout gridbag = new GridBagLayout( );
    GridBagConstraints c = new GridBagConstraints( );
    setLayout(gridbag);
    c.weightx = 1.0;
    newButton("One",gridbag,c);
    c.weightx = 4.0;
    newButton("Two",gridbag,c);
    c.gridwidth = GridBagConstraints.REMAINDER;
    newButton("Three", gridbag, c);
    }
}
```

The resulting buttons are shown in fig. 9.14.

Fig. 9.14 *Using the weightx instance variable for the GridBagLayout class.*

If the *gridwidth* is assigned to *GridBagConstraints.RELATIVE* the next component added is the next to last in the row. When the lines shown below are added to the previous example, fig. 9.15 is produced:

```
c.gridwidth = GridBagConstraints.RELATIVE;
NewButton("Four",gridbag,c);
c.gridwidth = GridBagConstraints.REMAINDER;
NewButton("Five",gridbag,c);
```

Note that the width assigned to the button with the label *Four* is equivalent to the width of the components in the above row, apart from the last component. The effect of this is that buttons *three* and *five* are the same width.

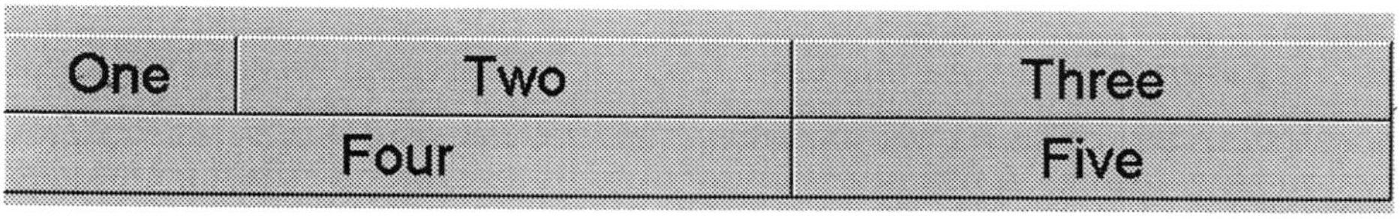

One	Two	Three
Four		Five

Fig. 9.15 *Using GridbagConstraints.REMAINDER.*

The *BorderLayout* class

The *BorderLayout* class is used to add components around the edges of the screen, or in the remainder area as shown in fig. 9.16.

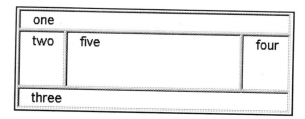

Fig. 9.16 *The BorderLayout class.*

The code needed to create this layout is shown below.

```
setLayout(new BorderLayout( ));
add("North", new TextField(" one "));
add("West", new TextField(" two "));
add("South", new TextField(" three "));
add("East", new TextField(" four "));
add("Center", new TextField(" five "));
```

The *setLayout* instruction specifies that this panel is using the *BorderLayout* class. The first parameter of the *add* method gives which of the five regions the method is referring to, this must be either *North, South, East, West* or *Center*. The *TextField* specifies the text which is to be put into the specified section of the panel.

You can specify gaps between the five sections by adding two additional parameters, which give the horizontal and vertical gap, for example:

```
setLayout(new BorderLayout(20,30));
```

The *CardLayout* class

Card layouts are used to display a sequence of panel layouts to provide a slide show type effect, for example:

```
setLayout(new CardLayout( ));
Panel theFirst = new Panel( );
Panel theSecond = new Panel( );
Panel theThird = new Panel( );
add("one", theFirst);
add("two", theSecond);
add("third", theThird);
```

This will create a three panel layout and add text to them using the *add* method.

You can specify the gaps between the horizontal and vertical gaps by adding two additional parameters as for the other layouts, for example:

```
setLayout(new CardLayout(20,30));
```

This layout class has a number of methods which are not shared with the other layout classes and so the main ones are given here:

Table 9.9 The methods of the CardLayout component.

Method	Description
first(Container)	Displays the first panel. That is the first panel created.
last(Container)	Displays the last panel.
next(Container)	Displays the next container in the sequence.
previous(Container)	Displays the previous container.
show(Container, String)	Displays the specified component in the specified container.

Layout methods

The following methods are found in all of the 5 layout classes:

Table 9.10 The methods of the layout components.

Method	Description
add(String, Component)	Adds the named component to the specified layout.
remove(Component)	Removes the specified component from the layout.
layoutContainer( )	This method reshapes the components in the container to meet the requirements of the *BorderLayout* object.
minimumLayoutSize(Container)	Returns the minimum dimensions needed to layout the components contained in the specified container.
preferredLayoutSize(Container)	Returns the ideal dimensions needed to layout the components contained in the specified container.

Using the layout managers

The five layout managers can be used to give you a professional looking applet, but until you have grown used to them, they can seem a bit awkward, particularly if you are used to using Visual Basic or Delphi for designing screen layouts. In this section we are going to look at how you would divide your page into three panels and give each panel a different appearance. The finished applet is shown in fig. 9.17.

In the initialisation routine the *GridLayout* manager is specified, while this does give less flexibility than the *GridBagLayout* manager, it is easier to use.

The first stage is to divide the working area into three vertical strips using the *GridLayout* manager:

```
setLayout(new GridLayout(1,3,10,10));
```

The three panels are created and displayed using the following code:

```
Panel panel1 = new Panel( );
add(panel1);
Panel panel2 = new Panel( );
add(panel2);
Panel panel3 = new Panel( );
add(panel3);
```

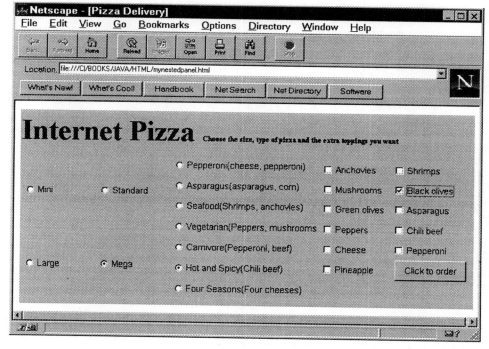

Fig. 9.17 *The pizza delivery application.*

The layout of each of the newly defined panels can be defined using another layout manager. In this case *panel1*, the leftmost panel is split into a two by two grid.

```
panel1.setLayout(new GridLayout(2,2,10,10));
```

The first component added to the grid goes into the top left corner, the second in the adjacent position on the right. The second row is filled next from left to right. A group of checkboxes are added which allow the size of the pizza to be specified. Note that these checkboxes are members of the same group called *sizegroup* and so only one of them may be selected at a time. Selecting a new checkbox automatically deselects all the others.

Similarly *panel2* is divided into seven rows and *panel3* is divided into a grid with seven rows and two columns. You can only select one type of pizza, but can add as many toppings as you wish.

Finally the header has to be added at the top of the page. This is specified in the *paint* method, using two different sized fonts. One important thing to remember is that you need to leave room for the heading to be displayed. This is done by specifying an inset from the edge of the page of 80 pixels at the top and 10 from each of the sides:

```
public Insets insets( ) {
    return new Insets(80,10,10,10);
}
```

The completed code looks like this:

```
import java.awt.*;
public class MyNestedPanel extends java.applet.Applet {

public void init( ) {
    setLayout(new GridLayout(1,3,10,10));
    Panel panel1 = new Panel( );
    add(panel1);
    Panel panel2 = new Panel( );
    add(panel2);
    Panel panel3 = new Panel( );
    add(panel3);
    panel1.setLayout(new GridLayout(2,2,10,10));
    CheckboxGroup sizegroup = new CheckboxGroup( );
    panel1.add(new Checkbox("Mini", sizegroup, false));
    panel1.add(new Checkbox("Standard", sizegroup, true));
    panel1.add(new Checkbox("Large", sizegroup, false));
    panel1.add(new Checkbox("Mega", sizegroup, false));
    panel2.setLayout(new GridLayout(7,1,10,10));
    CheckboxGroup t = new CheckboxGroup( );
    panel2.add(new Checkbox("Pepperoni(cheese,   pepperoni)",t, false));
    panel2.add(new Checkbox("Asparagus(asparagus, corn)", t, false));
    panel2.add(new Checkbox("Seafood(Shrimps, anchovies)", t, false));
    panel2.add(new Checkbox("Vegetarian(Peppers, mushrooms)", t,false));
    panel2.add(new Checkbox("Carnivore(Pepperoni, beef)",t, false));
    panel2.add(new Checkbox("Hot and Spicy(Chilli beef)",t,false));
    panel2.add(new Checkbox("Four Seasons(Four cheeses)", t, false));
    panel3.setLayout(new GridLayout(7,2));
    panel3.add(new Checkbox("Anchovies"));
    panel3.add(new Checkbox("Shrimps"));
    panel3.add(new Checkbox("Mushrooms"));
    panel3.add(new Checkbox("Black olives"));
    panel3.add(new Checkbox("Green olives"));
    panel3.add(new Checkbox("Asparagus"));
    panel3.add(new Checkbox("Peppers"));
```

```
        panel3.add(new Checkbox("Chilli beef"));
        panel3.add(new Checkbox("Cheese"));
        panel3.add(new Checkbox("Pepperoni"));
        panel3.add(new Checkbox("Pineapple"));
        panel3.add(new Button("Click here to order"));
        }
    public Insets insets( ) {
        return new Insets(80,10,10,10);
        }
    public void paint(Graphics g) {
        Font f = new Font("TimesRoman", Font.BOLD, 48);
        g.setFont(f);
        g.drawString("Internet Pizza", 1, 50);
        Font f1 = new Font("TimesRoman", Font.BOLD, 12);
        g.setFont(f1);
        g.drawString("Choose the size, type of pizza and the extra toppings you
        want", 300, 50);
        }
}
```

10

Handling Events

Introduction

We have looked at how the components in the *java.awt* package are used to design Web pages, but this is only part of the picture. The pages we have created do not do anything, there needs to be some code in the background which responds to the selecting of an item from a list or clicking on a button. These components have events associated with them, for example when you click on a button or select an item from a list an event occurs. In Java you can detect that event and take some action in response to it. The Java code that you write to deal with events are called event procedures. The event handlers for the mouse and the keyboard are members of the *java.awt.component* class.

In this chapter you will learn:

- How events occur.
- What the mouse events are.
- What the keyboard events are.
- How to use the *handleEvent* method for taking action when events occur.

Mouse events

The mouse can only generate a few different events which occur when it is clicked, moved or dragged. The mouse events that we are going to look at are:

- *mouseDown.*
- *mouseUp.*
- *mouseDrag.*
- *mouseMove.*
- *mouseEnter.*
- *mouseExit.*

The *mouseDown* and *mouseUp* events

When a mouse button is clicked, two events take place, *mouseDown* and *mouseUp*. If you want to take some action when one of these events occurs you have to add the corresponding method to your applet. These methods have the format:

> *public boolean mouseDown(Event evt, int x, int y) {*
>
> *....*
> *}*
>
> *public boolean mouseUp(Event evt, int x, int y) {*
>
> *....*
> *}*

The *Event* argument contains information about the event which has occurred. The other two arguments give the position of the mouse when the event occurred.

This simple applet displays a text field when it is run, the field disappears when the mouse button is pressed and appears when it is released, as shown in fig. 10.1.

   **Fig. 10.1** *Now you see me.*

Clicking on a mouse button is two separate events, *mouseDown* and *mouseUp*. When an event occurs, Java automatically executes the corresponding event handler.

> *import java.awt.*;*
> *public class MouseClick extends java.applet.Applet {*
>
> *TextField myText = new TextField(" Now you see me ");*
> *public void init( ) {*
> *add(myText);*
> *}*
>
> *public boolean mouseDown(Event evt, int x, int y) {*
> *myText.setText("");*
> *return true;*
> *}*
>
> *public boolean mouseUp(Event evt, int x, int y) {*
> *myText.setText(" Now you see me ");*
> *return true;*
> *}*
> *}*

Boolean methods

If you specify your own event handler in your applet you will override the default handler. All of the event handlers return a boolean value, (note the word *boolean* before the class name *mouseUp* and *mouseDown*). If *true* is returned then it is assumed that your method has dealt with the event successfully and that there is no need for the default handler to be used. If you return *false* then it is assumed that your handler has not dealt with the event.

The line drawing applet

This example draws lines on the screen. The start position of the line is when the mouse button is pressed (a *mouseUp* event occurs), and the end position when the mouse button is released (a *mouseDown* event occurs). The status of the mouse button and its co-ordinates are shown in a text box. The completed running applet is shown in fig. 10.2.

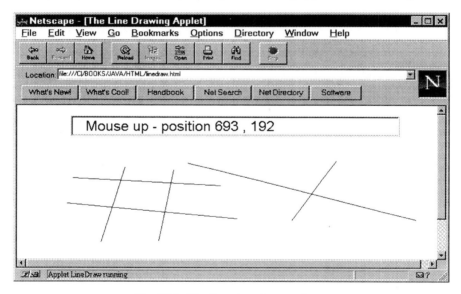

Fig. 10.2 The line drawing applet.

The lines are drawn using the *drawLine* method. This has the form:

  drawLine(int x1, int y1, int x2, int y2);

The four parameters are:

- The starting x and y co-ordinates of the line.
- The finishing x and y co-ordinates.

The *drawLine* method is called from the *paint* method. The *paint* method is called via the *repaint* method after the mouse button has been released. The only drawback with using the *repaint* method is that the screen is erased prior to drawing the specified object, so every time a new line is added to the display all the previous lines must be redrawn. Therefore a record of all the starting and finishing co-ordinates of all the previous points must be kept.

The *mouseDown* and *mouseUp* event handlers must be added. These supply the x and y co-ordinates of the mouse at the time the event occurs. The co-ordinates when the button is pressed give the start position of the line and the co-ordinates when it is released the end points.

The *Point* object is used to represent an x and a y co-ordinate. The statement below defines *start* as being an array of type *Point*:

Point start[ ] = new Point[max];

To reference, for example, the x co-ordinate of the first element refer to *start[0].x*. The y co-ordinate of for example, the fourth point is given by *start[3].y*. Note that arrays in Java start at zero.

- The *init* class is called when the applet is first run. It sets the background to white and creates a blank TextField.
- The *mouseDown* event handler displays the following message in the TextField *Mouse down - position* followed by the x and y co-ordinates of the mouse. The next free element of the *start* array is used to save the co-ordinates.
- The *mouseUp* method displays the message *Mouse up - position* followed by the x and y co-ordinates of the mouse. The finish position of the line is added to the *finish* array. The integer pointer, *sofar*, to the next free position in the *start* and *finish* arrays is incremented and the *repaint* method is called.
- The *paint* method, which is called indirectly via the *repaint* method, sets the colour of the lines to be drawn to black and draws all the lines, including the new one.

The completed code for this applet is given below:

```
import java.awt.*;
public class LineDraw extends java.applet.Applet {
    TextField myText = new TextField("",40);
    int max = 100;
    Point start[ ] = new Point[max];
    Point finish[ ] = new Point[max];
    int sofar = 0;

    public void init( ) {
        setBackground(Color.white);
        add(myText);
    }
    public boolean mouseDown(Event evt, int x, int y) {
        myText.setText(" Mouse down - position " + x + " , " + y);
        start[sofar] = new Point(x, y);
```

```
        return true;
    }
    public boolean mouseUp(Event evt, int x, int y) {
        myText.setText(" Mouse up - position " + x + " , " + y);
        finish[sofar] = new Point(x, y);
        sofar++;
        repaint( );
        return true;
    }
    public void paint(Graphics g) {
        int c;
        g.setColor(Color.black);
        for (c = 0; c < sofar; c++)
            drawLine(start[c].x,start[c].y, finish[c].x, finish[c].y);
    }
```

The *repaint* method is designed for animation, which is one of the main uses of Java, however as we have seen it does cause problems if you simply want to add anything to an existing screen. The next example, the scribble program looks at another way of dealing with this problem, the same technique could have been used in this example.

The scribble applet

The scribble applet draws a line on the screen which follows the movement of the mouse when it is dragged, that is when the mouse is moved with the button pressed.

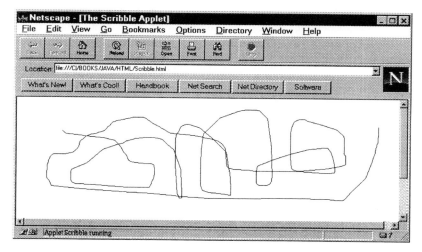

Fig. 10.3 *The scribble applet.*

The completed running applet is shown in fig. 10.3.

There is a problem here if we try and use the same approach as in the previous example, there are so many points that it is an enormous overhead to redraw all the lines every time a new one is added. The *repaint* method calls the *update* method which clears the screen. We need to add a new *update* method which overrides the default method, but which does not clear the screen, but simply calls the *paint* method.

The differences between this applet and the line drawing applet are:

- Only two points - *start* and *finish* - need to be declared, rather than an array.
- In the *mouseDrag* event, which occurs whenever the mouse is dragged, the previous position (*finish*) is copied to *start* and becomes the new starting point.
- The present co-ordinates of the mouse are used as the finishing points.
- The *repaint* method is called, which calls *update* which in turn calls *paint* which draws the line using the *drawLine* method.

The completed applet looks like this:

```
import java.awt.*;
public class Scribble extends java.applet.Applet {
Point start, finish;

public void init( ) {
    setBackground(Color.white);
    }
public boolean mouseDrag( Event evt, int x, int y) {
    start = finish;
    finish = new Point(x, y);
    repaint( );
    return true;
    }
public void update(Graphics g) {
    paint(g);
    }
public void paint(Graphics g) {
    g.setColor(Color.black);
    g.drawLine(start.x, start.y, finish.x, finish.y);
    }
}
```

If you try this applet you may find that the line drawn is not continuous. This is because the computer may not be able to process all the *mouseDrag* events fast enough and may miss some. The faster your computer the less likely this is to be a problem, however one way of reducing the problem is to amend your code to ignore one or two *mouseDrag* events, by changing the *mouseDrag* code as shown:

```
public boolean mouseDrag( Event evt, int x, int y) {
    if (c==2) {
        start = finish;
```

```
        finish = new Point(x, y);
        repaint( );
        c = 0;
        } else c++;
    return true;
    }
```

The integer variable *c* must be declared and initialised to zero when the applet is first run. If this does not solve the problem of disconnected lines you may need to ignore more than one in two *mouseDrag* events

Keyboard events

The keyboard events occur whenever a key is pressed. They are similar to the mouse events in the way in which Java deals with them. There are only two keyboard events:

- *keyDown.*
- *keyUp.*

The *keyDown* event handler looks like this:

```
    public boolean keyDown(Event Evt, int key) {
    }
```

The integer value gives the ASCII code for the key pressed.

There are some special keys which are defined to make it easier to deal with keys which are used to control cursor position on the screen, that is the arrowed, home, end page up and page down keys:

Table 10.1 *Keyboard events.*

Variable	Key pressed
Event.UP	Up arrow
Event.DOWN	Down arrow
Event.LEFT	Left arrow
Event.RIGHT	Right arrow
Event.PGUP	Page up
Event.PGDN	Page Down
Event.HOME	Home (leftmost position)
Event.END	End (rightmost position)

This applet moves an arrow around the screen in response to the pressing of the arrowed keys. The image of the arrow is changed depending on which arrow key is pressed. The gif files containing the arrows were created using CorelDraw!, but any similar drawing package could be used. The gif files are shown in fig 10.4.

- The background colour is set to white at initialisation time using the *setBackground* method.

- The *getImage* method is used to create four instances of an *Image* class, one for each of the four arrows. The initial arrow is pointing up.
- Depending on which of the arrowed keys is pressed, the image position is moved by changing either *xPos* or *yPos*. These values are supplied to the *drawImage* method which draws the new image.
- The *repaint* method calls the *update* method which erases the existing image and then calls the *paint* method which draws the new image.

right.gif   left.gif   up.gif   down.gif

Fig. 10.4 *The four gif files.*

```
import java.awt.*;
public class Keyboard extends java.applet.Applet {
    Image temp, up, down, left, right;
    int xPos, yPos;

    public void init( ) {
        setBackground(Color.white);
        up = getImage(getCodeBase( ),"up.gif");
        down = getImage(getCodeBase( ),"down.gif");
        left = getImage(getCodeBase( ),"left.gif");
        right = getImage(getCodeBase( ),"right.gif");
        temp = up;
        xPos = 200;
        yPos = 200;
    }

    public boolean keyDown(Event evt, int x) {
        switch (x) {
            case Event.UP
                yPos -= 10;
                temp = up;
                break
            case Event.DOWN
                yPos += 10;
                temp = down;
                break;
            case Event.LEFT
                xPos -= 10;
                temp = left;
                break;
```

```
                    case Event.RIGHT
                        xPos += 10;
                        temp = right;
                        }
                    break;
                }
            repaint( );
            return true;
            }

            public void paint(Graphics g) {
                g.drawImage(temp, xPos, yPos, 40, 40, this);
                }
            }
```

A full description of using existing images in Java applets is given in chapter 6.

The *handleEvent* method

In this chapter we have looked at handling mouse and keyboard events, but these are
special cases, whenever an event occurs in Java you can handle the event by overriding
the default method called *handleEvent*. The name of the event which has occurred is
passed to this method and you can test for specific events to see which one has occurred
and so take different actions for different events.

In the previous example an arrow was driven around the page using the four arrowed
keys, this was done using the *keyDown* method, but the same could be achieved using
the *handleEvent* method (and omitting the *keyDown* method) as shown below:

```
    public boolean handleEvent(Event evt) {
        switch (evt.id) {
            case Event.MOUSE_UP:
                yPos -= 10;
                temp = up;
                break;
            case Event.MOUSE_DOWN:
                yPos += 10;
                temp = up;
                break;
            case Event.MOUSE_LEFT:
                yPos -= 10;
                temp = up;
                break;
            case Event.MOUSE_RIGHT:
                yPos += 10;
                temp = up;
                break;
```

```
        default:
            return false;
        }
    repaint( );
    return true;
    }
```

The *Event* object is provided and can be used to distinguish between the different events which have occurred. The event identifier is an integer which can be compared against the event identifiers defined in the *Event* class. Some of the more common ones are listed in table 10.2:

Table 10.2 *Commonly used events.*

Event identifier	Event identifier	Event identifier
ALT_MASK	UP	MOUSE_UP
SHIFT_MASK	DOWN	MOUSE_DOWN
CTRL_MASK	LEFT	MOUSE_MOVE
HOME	RIGHT	MOUSE DRAG
END	WINDOW_MOVED	MOUSE_ENTER
PGUP	KEY_PRESS	MOUSE_EXIT
PGDN	KEY_RELEASE	

The events are clear from their names, with the exception of MOUSE_ENTER and MOUSE_EXIT which occur when the mouse enters and leaves the area on the page allocated to the applet.

The *action* method

The same event can be caused by more than one component, if, for example, there are two buttons then the *handleEvent* method cannot be used to tell which button has been pressed, since it does not have this information available. If you do need to distinguish between buttons you need to use the *action* method.

The *action* method looks like this:

```
public boolean action(Event evt, Object arg) {
    if (evt.target instanceof Button) {
        buttonHandler((String)arg);
        return true;
        }
    else return false;
    }
```

The first argument of the *action* method is the object which originated the event. The second argument can be any sort of object, depending on the originating object. For buttons this argument is the label on the button. For text boxes the argument is the text in the textbox. For menus the argument is the text of the menu item.

In the next example, we are going to use the *action* method to detect which of two buttons has been pressed and to change the size of some text. The working applet is shown in fig. 10.5.

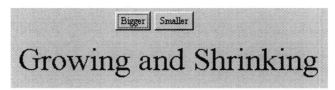

Fig. 10.5 The action method.

In the *init* method the two buttons and the text are created. The *size* variable is the initial size of the text.

```
public void init( ) {
    size = 10;
    add(new Button("Bigger"));
    add(new Button("Smaller"));
}
```

The first line in the *action* method, shown below, tests the type of object that caused the event. This object is stored in the events target instance variable. In this example a check is made to see if the object is a button.

```
public boolean action(Event evt, Object arg) {
    if (evt.target instanceof Button) {
        buttonHandler((String)arg);
        return true;
    }
    else return false;
}
```

Since this method is called for every event that occurs (unless you have provided your own specific handler for mouse and keyboard events) it is not good practice to place all the code for dealing with the event in this method. For this reason if the object is a button the *buttonHandler* method is called. The string which is passed to this method is the text on the button. By testing for the text smaller and bigger you can determine which button has been pressed.

Note that if the event which caused the event was a button, *true* is returned from the *action* method. All other events cause *false* to be returned, indicating that some action may need to be taken by the default handlers.

The full listing is shown below:

```
public class GrowingAndShrinking extends java.applet.Applet {
    int size;
```

```
public void init( ) {
    size = 10;
    add(new Button("Bigger"));
    add(new Button("Smaller"));
}

public boolean action(Event evt, Object arg) {
    if (evt.target instanceof Button) {
        buttonHandler((String)arg);
        return true;
    }
    else return false;
}

public void buttonHandler(String label) {
    if (label.equals("Bigger")) size +=5;
    else if (label.equals("Smaller")) size -=5;
    repaint( );
}

public void paint(Graphics g) {
    Font thefont = new Font("TimesRoman", Font.PLAIN, size);
    g.setFont(thefont);
    g.drawString("Growing and Shrinking", 130, 80);
}
}
```

11

Windows, Dialogs and Menus

Introduction

Windows, dialog boxes and menus have become a standard part of virtually all applications, particularly if you are working in a Windows 95 environment. The *Window* class in Java allows you to control and manipulate windows. Dialog boxes are a special form of window, which have less functionality than a standard window.

Windows can have their own menu bar, which must be at the top of the window and have a higher level of functionality, including minimise and maximise buttons.

In this chapter, you will learn about:

- Using windows.
- Using dialog boxes.
- Creating menus.

Creating and displaying windows

The *Window* class has two subclasses:

- The *Frame* subclass allows you to create windows and menu bars.
- The *Dialog* subclass allows you to create dialog boxes.

To create a frame without a heading use the following constructor:

new Frame( );

To create a frame with a heading, you need to specify a parameter:

new Frame(String);

After you have created a frame, more commonly called a window, you have to make it visible, you do this with the *show* method, for example:

myWindow = new Frame("Java window");
myWindow.show( );

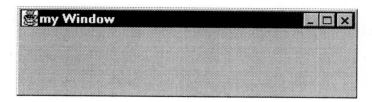

Fig. 11.1 *A Java window.*

The window has the usual Windows 95 features for minimising, maximising and closing as shown in fig. 11.1.

Some environments may display a prominent message saying *Untrusted Java Applet Window,* which may initially make you think that there is a problem. This is a not an error, it is a feature of the browser and tells users that the window is being created by a Java applet and not by the browser. It is intended to be a security measure and cannot be turned off.

Adding objects to pages

In addition to adding objects such as list boxes and buttons directly to a Web page you can add them to windows. In this example we create a window, divide it into two panels, with different layout managers and add a label and button to the window. The running applet is shown in fig. 11.2.

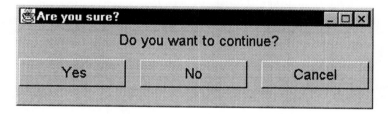

Fig. 11.2 *Adding objects to windows.*

A frame is created which has the title *are you sure?* It is then assigned the *GridLayout* manager with two horizontal grids:

```
window = new Frame("Are you sure? ");
window.setLayout(new GridLayout(2,1,10,10));
```

The first grid square has a label added to it. The second grid square has a panel added to it which is divided into three horizontal grid squares and a button added to each:

```
window.add(new Label("Do you want to continue? "));
Panel panel1 = new Panel( );
panel1.setLayout(new GridLayout(1,3,20,20));
window.add(panel1);
```

```
panel1.add(new Button(" Yes "));
panel1.add(new Button(" No "));
panel1.add(new Button(" Cancel "));
```

Finally the window is displayed by the *show* method:

```
window.show( );
```

The complete applet listing is shown below:

```
import java.applet.Applet;
import java.awt.*;
public class AddingObjects extends java.applet.Applet {
    Frame window;
    Button Button1, Button2, Button3;

    public void init( ) {
        window = new Frame("Are you sure? ");
        window.setLayout(new GridLayout(2,1,10,10));
        window.add(new Label("Do you want to continue? "));
        Panel panel1 = new Panel( );
        panel1.setLayout(new GridLayout(1,3,20,20));
        window.add(panel1);
        panel1.add(new Button(" Yes "));
        panel1.add(new Button(" No "));
        panel1.add(new Button(" Cancel"));
        window.resize(100,50);
        window.show( );
    }
}
```

If you want to make a window invisible, use the *hide* method.

If you want to change the default font in a panel use the *setFont* method, for example, after creating *panel1* add the following two lines of code:

```
Font theFont = new Font(Arial",Font.PLAIN,20);
panel1.setFont(theFont)
```

If you want to take some action in response to the pressing of a button you can use the event handlers covered in chapter 10.

Menus

An integral feature of windows is that a window can have a menu, which can drop down to give a number of options as shown in fig. 11.3

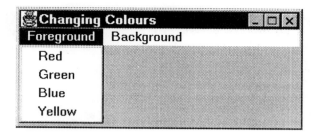

Fig. 11.3 Adding objects to windows.

The first stage is to create a menubar, that is a new instance of the class *MenuBar*:

> *MenuBar m = new MenuBar( );*

Next menu headers are added to the menu bar:

> *Menu mFor = new Menu("Foreground");*
> *m.add(mFor);*

Finally menu items are added to the menu headers:

> *mFor.add(new MenuItem("Red"));*

The complete code is shown below:

```
public void init( ) {
    window = new Frame("Changing Colours");
    MenuBar m = new MenuBar( );
    Menu mFor = new Menu("Foreground");
    m.add(mFor);
    mFor.add(new MenuItem("Red"));
    mFor.add(new MenuItem("Green"));
    mFor.add(new MenuItem("Blue"));
    mFor.add(new MenuItem("Yellow"));
    m.add(mBack);
    Menu mBack = new Menu("Background");
    mBack.add(new MenuItem("White"));
    mBack.add(new MenuItem("Black"));
    window.setMenuBar(m);
    window.show( );
}
public boolean action(Event evt, Object arg) {
    if (evt.target instanceof MenuItem) {
        String label = (String)arg;
        if (label.equals("Red")) setForeground(Color.red);
        else if (label.equals("Green")) setForeground(Color.green);
        else if (label.equals("Blue")) setForeground(Color.blue);
        else if (label.equals("Yellow")) setForeground(Color.yellow);
        else if (label.equals("White")) setBackground(Color.white);
```

```
        else if (label.equals("Black")) setBackground(Color.black);
        }
repaint( );
return true;
        }
}
```

Types of menu items

In addition to adding menu items to menus there are three other types of items that you can add to menus:

- Separators. A separator is a line dividing menu items into groups.
- Submenus.
- Checked menu items.

If you want to add a separator, just make the text for the new menu item a "-" character, for example:

```
window = new Frame("Creating Submenus");
MenuBar m = new MenuBar( );
Menu mFile = new Menu("Font");
m.add(mFile);
mFile.add(new MenuItem("Times Roman"));
mFile.add(new MenuItem("Courier"));
mFile.add(new MenuItem("Helvetica"));
mFile.add(new MenuItem("-"));
mFile.add(new MenuItem("Size"));
```

The resulting menu is shown in fig. 11.4

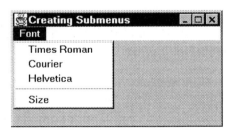

Fig. 11.4 Separator lines in menus.

If you want to add a submenu, perhaps to offer a range of font sizes, you do this by adding an instance of *Menu* to the *mFile* menu and then adding new items to that menu. In the example below, a new menu called *mSize* is created, and added to the *mFile* menu. Items are then added to the *mSize* menu.

```
Menu mSize = new Menu("Size");
mFile.add(mSize);
mSize.add(new MenuItem("8"));
mSize.add(new MenuItem("10"));
mSize.add(new MenuItem("12"));
```

The new menu system is shown in fig. 11.5

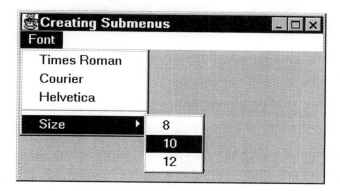

Fig. 11.5 *Creating submenus.*

The final type of menu item that you can add is an instance of the *CheckboxMenuItem* class (rather than the *MenuItem* class). This item has a checkbox against its text indicating whether is on or off. Successive clicks on this item toggle its state, for example:

```
mFor.add(new CheckboxMenuItem("Show status bar"));
mFor.add(new CheckboxMenuItem("Show vertical ruler"));
mFor.add(new CheckboxMenuItem("Show horizontal ruler"));
```

This menu system is shown in fig. 11.6.

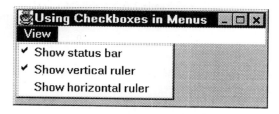

Fig. 11.6 *The CheckboxMenuItem class.*

The *CheckboxMenu* class should only be used when a menu item can be toggled on or off. Toggling one instance of this class to "on" does not automatically turn other instances "off". As you would expect these items behave like checkboxes and not like a group of radio boxes where only one of the group may be "on".

Enabling and disabling menu items

Sometimes you want to indicate that a menu item is not available. You can do this using the *disable* method as shown in fig. 11.7 to disable the *Paste* menu item. *Paste* is not an allowable option unless something has been cut or copied.:

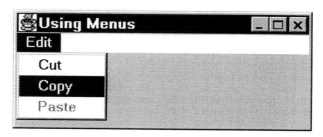

Fig. 11.7 Disabling menu items.

The disabled menu item is shown as a lighter shade than enabled items.

```
Menu mEdit = new Menu("Edit");
m.add(mEdit);
mEdit.add(new MenuItem("Cut"));
mEdit.add(new MenuItem("Copy"));
MenuItem mPaste = new MenuItem("Paste");
mEdit.add(mPaste);
mPaste.disable( );
```

You can make a menu item which has been disabled available again using the *enable* method.

The *Dialog* subclass

Dialog boxes are similar to frames except that they do not have the same degree of functionality as frames.

- Dialog boxes do not have menus.
- Dialog boxes are usually modal (that is the applet cannot proceed until you have responded to it).
- Dialog boxes must be attached to a frame, they cannot exist independently.
- Dialog boxes use fewer system resources.

If you want to display a temporary window, perhaps giving a warning, you should use a dialog box rather than a frame.

There are two constructors for dialog boxes:

- *Dialog(Frame, boolean).*
- *Dialog(Frame, String, boolean).*

The *boolean* argument is true if the form is modal, this is usually the case for dialogs.

The *String* argument is optional. It is the text that is placed on the title bar. If you omit this argument the dialog will not have a title bar.

In the next example, an instance of the *Dialog* class is created:

> *warningDialog = new Dialog(window, "Warning", true);*

This is divided into two vertical grid squares. The top grid square has a label added to it:

> *warningDialog.setLayout(new GridLayout(2,1,10,10));*
> *warningDialog.add(new Label("Are you sure? ",Label.CENTER));*

The lower of the two grid squares has a panel added to it and is divided into two grid squares, each containing a *Button* component.

> *Panel panel1 = new Panel( );*
> *warningDialog.add(panel1);*
> *panel1.setLayout(new GridLayout(1,2,40,40));*
> *panel1.add(new Button(" Yes "));*
> *panel1.add(new Button(" No "));*

The window produced by this applet is shown in fig 11.8.

This will create the dialog box, but not display it. You need to use the *show* method to do this:

> *warningDialog.show( );*

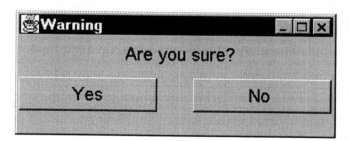

Fig. 11.8 Dialog boxes.

To hide the dialog box use the *hide* method:

> *warningDialog.hide( );*

Windows methods

The most common methods of the *Window* class are shown in table 11.1.

Table 11.1 *Common methods of the Window class.*

Method	Description
dispose	Destroys the window releasing all system resources.
show	Displays the window.
toBack	Sends the frame to the back of the window.
toFront	Sends the frame to the front of the window.

In addition the *frame* subclass has the following useful methods:

Table 11.2 *Methods of the Frame class.*

Method	Description
hide	Makes the frame invisible.
getTitle	Returns the title of the frame.
getMenuBar	Returns the menu bar for the frame.
isResizable	Returns true if the frame can be resized.
remove(MenuComponent)	Removes the specified menu bar from the frame.
setMenuBar(MenuBar)	Sets the menu bar for this frame the menu bar specified.
setResizable(boolean)	If the boolean is true, frame resizing is allowed.
setTitle(String)	Sets the title of the frame to the specified string.

The *Dialog* subclass does not have many of the methods of the *Frame* class, in particular the only two of the methods listed in table 11.2 which the *Dialog* class does have are the *isResizable* and the *setResizable* methods.

12

Input and Output Streams

Introduction

If you have a UNIX background you are likely to be familiar with the concept of streams. A stream is a continuous flow of bytes that can come from any source, such as the Internet, another program or more commonly a file. Streams can be used for input or for output from your application or applet.

In this chapter you will learn about:

- Input streams.
- Output streams.
- Stream exceptions.

Java is designed primarily to be a language for providing interactive Web pages that can be run using any computer system which supports a browser with a Java interpreter. One of the problems that this can cause is that the applet does not know anything about the file organisation on the host system. Attempts to read or write files are therefore likely to cause problems. Even attempts to write a file and then read it are likely to fail due to violation of the security system on the host computer. If you are writing applications which run locally these problems will not arise. Most of the examples in this chapter, especially those which deal with files, are applications rather than applets to ensure that the examples will work correctly without problems.

The *java.io* package

The *java.io* package contains all the classes required for dealing with streams. All the input streams are members of the abstract class *java.io.InputStream*. There are six subclasses of *InputStream*:

- *FileInputStream.*
- *ByteArrayInputStream.*
- *StringBufferInputStream.*

- *FilterInputStream.*
- *PipedInputStream.*
- *SequenceInputStream.*

In addition the *FilterInputStream* class has four subclasses:

- *BufferedInputStream.*
- *DataInputStream.*
- *LineNumberInputStream.*
- *PushbackInputStream.*

All of these streams will block when reading, that is they will wait for input. Since Java supports multithreading the system resources are available to do other things while this thread is waiting.

We look at each of these classes and subclasses in turn.

The *FileInputStream* class

The *FileInputStream* class is used when the input stream is a file. There are three different constructors for this class. In the simplest the file name is specified as a string, for example:

> *InputStream s = new FileInputStream("myfile.txt");*

However there are also two other forms. The first uses the *File* class, for example:

> *File myfile = new File("myfile.txt");*
> *InputStream s = new FileInputStream(myfile);*

The third uses a file descriptor from a file which had been opened earlier, for example:

> *InputStream s = newFileInputStream("myfile.txt");*
> *FileDesc = s.getFD( );*
> *s.close( );*
> *InputStream t = newFileInputStream(fileDesc);*

In this example the file *myfile.txt* is opened as stream *s*. Its file descriptor is found using the *getFD* method. Finally *myfile.txt* is opened again using the file descriptor. Sometimes it is useful to have more than one stream for the same file, when two sections are being read, it is not necessary to keep on changing the file pointer.

To see how this works in practice we look at an example which opens a text file and finds out how large it is.

First you need to import the *java.io package*. The start of the application looks like this:

> *import java.io.*;*
> *class FileToScreen {*
>   *public static void main (String argv[ ]) {*

Next the stream is defined:

```
InputStream s;
s = new FileInputStream("myfile.txt");
```

To find the size of the file in bytes the *available* method is used. The completed program looks like this:

```
import java.io.*;
class FileToScreen {
    public static void main (String argv[ ]) {
        int fileSize = -1;
        InputStream s;
        s = new FileInputStream("myfile.txt");
        fileSize = s.available( );
        System.out.print("File size is " + fileSize + " bytes\n");
        s.close( );
    }
}
```

It is good practice to close streams - not just file streams - to free up system resources when the stream is no longer needed. If you forget, the system is likely to do it for you when the application or applet ends, but you may have tied up scarce resources (such as memory) in the meantime, and there are no guarantees if you do not know what the host computer is. It is good practice to use the *finally* clause to close streams:

```
finally {
    s.close;
}
```

It is guaranteed that this clause will execute even if exceptions occur.

If you try to compile this application you will run into problems. The compiler informs you that you need to either catch or throw two exceptions which could occur when the program is run. The two exceptions are *FileNotFoundException* and *IOException*. It is best to catch these exceptions. You do this by enclosing the code where the exceptions can occur by a *try* statement and following the *try* clause by *catch* statements. The *IOException* class is a superclass of the *FileNotFoundException* class. If you list more than one *catch* clause in your application the first one which applies will be acted on. Therefore, if you list the *IOException* catch clause first, the *FileNotFoundException* clause will never be reached, therefore they must be listed the other way round. The completed program looks like this:

```
import java.io.*;
class FileToScreen {
public static void main (String argv[ ]) {
    int fileSize = -1;
    InputStream s;
    try {
        s = new FileInputStream("myfile.txt");
```

```
        fileSize = s.available( );
        System.out.print("File size is " + fileSize + " bytes\n");
        }
        catch (FileNotFoundException FNF) {
            System.out.println("\nFile not found");
        }
        catch (IOException IOE) {
            System.out.println("\nIO Exception");
        }
    }
}
```

Reading from streams

One of the most important set of methods relating to input streams which deal with reading data is the *read* method. There are three forms of the *read* method.

You can read a single byte at a time, for example, to read from the stream *s*:

```
        c = s.read( );
```

To read a series of bytes into an array:

```
        bytes myBuffer = new byte[100];
        InputStream s = new FileInputStream("myfile.txt");
        numberRead = s.read(myBuffer);
```

This will attempt to read 100 bytes (the size of *myBuffer*) from the stream. If it does this successfully, *numberRead* will be assigned the value 100. If less than 100 are read, because the end of the file is reached, *numberRead* will be assigned the actual number of bytes read from the stream.

You can also read a specified number of bytes to be read from an offset into the file, for example:

```
        numberRead = s.read(myBuffer, 10, 50);
```

This will read 50 bytes starting at byte 10. *numberRead* gives the actual number of bytes read.

Whenever the *read* method returns a value of -1 it indicates that no bytes have been read and the end of the stream has been reached. It does not indicate an error. When an error occurs in reading or writing, an exception is produced.

The *skip* and *mark* methods

Java also offers a few other useful methods for reading from streams. If you want to move forward to a new position in the stream you can use the *skip* method:

```
        bytesSkipped = skip(10);
```

This will move the stream pointer 10 bytes forward from the present position. The return value *bytesSkipped* gives the actual number of bytes skipped which may be less than the number required if the end of the stream is reached.

All of the methods we have looked at so far in this chapter are available for the *InputStream* class. The *mark* and *reset* methods are not available for all subclasses, but are available for the *FileInputStream* class. These two methods provide a way of marking a specified position in a stream and returning to that position later. Not all streams support this, but you can find out if the stream you are working with does support it by using the *markSupported* method, for example for a stream called *s*:

> *if (s.markSupported( )) mark(limit);*

The *markSupported* method returns a boolean which is true if *mark* and *reset* are supported.

The *mark* method has a single parameter, *limit* in the example above which is the maximum number of bytes you can move on from the current position before this mark position becomes invalid. Since all of the bytes from the marked position to any new position have to be stored this provides a way of limiting the size of this storage, which may take up large amounts of memory.

When you want to return to the marked position use the *reset* method:

> *s.reset( );*

You can only have one marked position.

The *ByteArrayInputStream* class

This class allows a buffer to be used as an *InputStream*:

> *byte[ ] myBuffer = new byte[100];*
> ...
> ...
> *InputStream s = new ByteArrayInputStream(myBuffer);*

This example defines an array of 100 bytes as an input stream. You can assign values to the array in any way you wish, by using assignment statements. You can use the *available*, *read*, *reset* and *skip* methods with this class.

- The *available* method is simply the size of the buffer.
- The *reset* method always returns the stream pointer to the start of the stream.

The *StringBufferInputStream* class

This class behaves in exactly the same way as the *ByteArrayStringInput* class except that is it used with streams of characters rather than streams of bytes.

The *FilterInputStream* class

There are four subclasses to the *FilterInputStream* class:

- *BufferedInputStream.*
- *DataInputStream.*
- *LineNumberInputStream.*
- *PushbackInputStream.*

The *FilterInputStream* class provides additional functionality for all the methods of the *InputStream* class. The effect of this will become apparent as we look at each of the subclasses in turn.

The *BufferedInputStream* class

This class allows you to read in characters from a stream without performing a read every time. Data is read into a buffer so that it is available the next time a read is requested. This is particularly useful if you are reading from a source which is inherently slow compared to the speed of the computer, such as a disk file or a source across the network.

```
InputStream s = new FileInputStream("myfile.txt");
b = new BufferedInputStream(s);
numberRead = b.read(myBuffer);
```

The first two lines could be more concisely written:

```
b = new BufferedInputStream(new FileInputStream("myfile.txt"));
```

You can now use the methods such as *read, available, mark* and *reset*. The benefit of using the *BufferedInputStream* class is improved performance when reading data. If you are performing repeated reads, much of the time, the data requested will be available in the buffer, and there is no need to go to the source of the stream.

You can specify the size of the buffer rather than relying on defaults by specifying an additional parameter:

```
b = new BufferedInputStream(s,2048);
```

This statement specifies a buffer size of 2048 bytes.

The *DataInputStream* class

The streams that we have looked at so far have been streams of bytes or characters. This stream supports methods that allow you to read the primitive data types, for example booleans and integers. The full list of these methods is shown in table 12.1.

Table 12.1 *Methods for the DataInputStream class.*

Method	Description
read(byte[ ])	Reads into an array of bytes.
read(byte[ ], int start , int len)	Reads into an array of bytes, the staring point and number of bytes to be read are specified.
readBoolean( )	Reads a boolean.
readByte( )	Reads a byte.
readChar( )	Reads a 16 bit character.
readDouble( )	Reads a 64 bit double integer.
readFloat( )	Reads a 32 bit floating point number.
readFully(byte[ ])	Reads bytes into an array until all the bytes are read.
readFully(byte[ ], int start , int len)	Reads bytes into an array until either all bytes or the required number are read whichever is first. The starting point and the number of bytes to be read are given.
readInt( )	Reads a 32 bit integer.
readLine( )	Reads a line terminated by \n, \r, \r\n or EOF.
readLong( )	Reads a 64 bit long integer.
readShort( )	Reads a 16 bit short integer.
readUTF( )	Reads a string in UTF format.
readUnsignedByte( )	Reads an unsigned 8 bit byte
readUnsignedShort( )	Reads an unsigned 16 bit integer
skipBytes(int)	Skips the specified number of bytes.

The code below will create an input stream from the file *myfile.txt* and read a floating point number from it.

```
InputStream d = new DataInputStream(new FileInputStream("myfile.txt"));
float myFloat = d.readFloat( );
```

The *LineNumberInputStream* class

This class has additional methods that keep a track of the current line number. The problem is that this class does not implement the *readLine* method, so the stream cannot be read a line at a time. This class is usually used in conjunction with the *DataInputStream* class which does have the *readLine* method. The next example shows how you can combine the *DataInputStream* and *LineNumberInputStream* classes:

```
LineNumberInputStream ln;
```

```
ln = new LineNumberInputStream(new FileInputStream("myfile.txt"));
DataInputStream d = new DataInputStream(ln);
for (c=0; c < 5; c++) {
    myLine = d.readLine( );
    lineNumber = ln.getLineNumber( );
    System.out.println("Line " + lineNumber + myLine);
}
```

In this example, the first five lines of *myfile.txt* are read and displayed. Each line is preceded by the text *Line* and the number of that line. It is the *FileInputStream* which is actually providing the data. The role of the *DataInputStream* is to provide buffered input of the data, while the *LineNumberInputStream* can be used to keep a record of which line of data is being read.

The *PushbackInputStream* class

The key feature of this class is the *unread* method which allows the stream pointer to be pushed back by one byte, so that a character is unread. The next time a byte is read the previously unread character will be returned. This is like a simpler version of the *mark*, *reset* methods:

```
s = new PushbackInputStream(new FileInputStream("myfile.txt"));
s.read( );
...
s.unread( );
```

The *PipedInputStream* class

In UNIX systems there is a concept called a pipe which allows a stream of bytes to be directed from one application to another. The *PipedInputStream* class implements this concept in Java to provide a straightforward way for threads to exchange data.

```
PipedInputStream input = PipedInputStream( );
```

This stream can be picked up by a corresponding piped output stream:

```
PipedOutputStream output = PipedOutputStream(input );
```

The *SequenceInputStream* class

This class allows you to take two input streams and combine them to a single stream:

```
InputStream head, body;
head = new FileInputStream("head.txt");
```

body = new FileInputStream("body.txt");
s = new SequenceInputStream(head, body);

The stream, *s*, behaves as if it were a single stream. When reading from this stream, if the end of the *head* stream is reached, the *body* stream is automatically read. This is particularly useful in situations where you have a standard header stream and a variety of different streams for the main body of the stream.

The *OutputStream* class

For every input stream there is an equivalent output stream.

The key difference is that the output streams support a set of write methods rather than the read methods of the *InputStream* class.

The five methods of the *OutputStream* class are:

Table 12.2 *Methods of the OutputStream class.*

Method	Description
close( )	Closes the stream and releases any resources held by the stream.
flush( )	Empties the buffer and writes any output bytes.
write(byte)	Writes the specified byte to the stream.
write(byte[ ]);	Writes all the bytes in the byte array.
write(byte[ ], int start, int size)	Writes *size* bytes from the byte array beginning at the *start* position.

All of the *write* methods will block, that is wait until the data is written. They behave in a similar way to the read methods of the *InputStream* class which also block until the data is read.

The *FileOutputStream* class

The *FileOutputStream* class is used when the output stream is a file; it is the companion of the *FileInputStream* class and many of the remarks made about that class, particularly those that relate to the problems of security violations, apply to this one. There are three different constructors for this class. In the simplest the file name is specified as a string, for example:

OutputStream s = new FileOutputStream("myfile.txt");

The second form uses the *File* class, for example:

File myfile = new File("myfile.txt");
OutputStream s = new FileOutputStream(myfile);

The third uses a file descriptor from a file which had been opened earlier, for example:

```
InputStream s = new FileOutputStream("myfile.txt");
FileDesc = s.getFD( );
s.close( );
OutputStream t = new  FileOutputStream(fileDesc);
```

In this example the file *myfile.txt* is opened as stream s. Its file descriptor is found using the *getFD* method. Finally *myfile.txt* is opened again using the file descriptor.

To see how this works in practice we look at an example which opens a text file for reading and writes the contents to an output file.

The body of the program without the exception handling looks like this:

```
InputStream input;
OutputStream output;
input = new FileInputStream("myfile.txt");
output = new FileOutputStream("outfile.txt");
fileSize = input.available( );
input.read(buffer);
output.write(buffer);
input.close( );
output.close( );
```

If you try this program remember to import the *java.io* package. You do need to be prepared to deal with the IO exceptions which may be caused by using these methods. You can either throw them or use the *try* and *catch* clauses to deal with them. You need to enclose the section of the application which is performing the IO within a *try* clause and then add the following *catch* clauses:

```
catch (FileNotFoundException FNF) {
    System.out.println("\nFile not found");
}
catch (IOException IOE) {
    System.out.println("\nIO Exception");
}
```

If an exception does occur, the appropriate error message will be displayed.

Writing to streams

We have already seen one example of writing to a file, in this section we are going to look at writing to files in more detail.

One of the most important set of methods relating to input streams deals with reading data. In the *FileInputStream* class there are three forms of the *read* method, similarly there are three forms of the *write* method for the *FileOutputStream* class.

You can write a single byte at a time, for example, to write from the stream *output*:

```
c = output.read( );
```

To write a series of bytes into an array:

> *bytes myBuffer = new byte[1024];*
> *OutputStream output = new FileOutputStream("myfile.txt");*
> *numberWritten = output.read(myBuffer);*

This will attempt to write 1024 bytes (the size of *myBuffer*) to the stream. If it does this successfully, *numberWritten* will be assigned the value 1024. If less than 1024 are written, perhaps because the disk is full or the user has used up his allocation of space on the network, *numberWritten* will be assigned the actual number of bytes written to the stream.

You can also write a specified number of bytes to be written from an input array, for example:

> *numberWritten = output.write(myBuffer, 10, 50);*

This will attempt to write 50 bytes starting at byte 10 in the *myBuffer* array to the output stream. The value of *numberWritten* gives the actual number of bytes written to the stream.

The *ByteArrayOutputStream* class

This class directs an output stream into a buffer;

> *byte[ ] myBuffer = new byte[1024];*
> ...
> ...
> *OutputStream s = newByteArrayOuputStream(myBuffer);*

This example defines an array of 1024 bytes as an output stream. Alternatively you do not have to specify the size of the output stream. You can just allow it to grow as more information is written to it:

> *OutputStream s = newByteArrayOuputStream( );*
> ...
> ...
> *s.write(value);*

Two useful methods are size and reset:

- The *size( )* method returns the size of the buffer, this will be the number of bytes written if the size of the buffer has not been explicitly declared.
- The *reset( )* method resets the buffer so that the next *write* statement will overwrite the data already written.

The *FilterOutputStream* class

There are three subclasses to the *FilterOutputStream* class:

- *BufferedOutputStream.*

- *PrintStream.*
- *DataOutputStream.*

The *FilterOutputStream* class provides additional functionality for all the methods of the *OutputStream* class. The effect of this will become apparent as we look at each of the subclasses in turn.

The *BufferedOutputStream* class

This stream is the converse of the *BufferedInputStream* class. It allows you to write characters to a stream without a write being executed every time. The data goes into a buffer. When the buffer is full or flushed, the data is written. The use of buffered output gives a marked improvement in performance when you are writing to relatively slow physical devices such as local disks or across a network.

```
OutputStream s = new FileOutputStream("outputFile.txt");
b = new BufferedOutputStream(s);
b.write(99);
```

Alternatively the first two lines could be more concisely written:

```
b = new BufferedOutputStream(new FileOutputStream("outputFile.txt"));
```

The *PrintStream* class

This output stream has a set of additional methods for printing. The stream is flushed every time a newline character is written to the stream.

We have already seen the most common methods *print* and *println* several times, for example:

```
System.out.print("hello");
System.out.println(" everyone");
System.out.println("hello everyone");
```

This will print *hello everyone* twice, on two separate lines.

The *print* and *println* methods behave in exactly the same way except that *println* moves to the start of a new line after printing. There are several variants on the print method which are listed in table 12.3.

These can be combined to print a series of any of the primitive Java types, for example:

```
String myString "The answer is ";
System.out.print(myString + answer);
```

There is a corresponding *println* method for each of the *print* methods.

Table12.3 *The print object.*

Method	Description
print(object)	Prints the specified object.
print(String)	Prints a string.
print(char[ ])	Print an array of characters. The top 8-bits of the 16-bit characters are discarded.
print(char)	Prints a single character.
print(int)	Prints an 32 bit integer.
print(long)	Prints a 64 bit integer.
print(float)	Prints a 32 bit floating point value.
print(double)	Prints a 64 bit integer.
print(boolean)	Prints a boolean value.

The *DataOutputStream* class

This is the converse of the *DataInputStream* class and as you would expect allows you to write the Java primitive data types rather than just bytes or characters.

The code below will create an output stream from the file *my.txt* and write a floating point number to it:

```
OutputStream d = new DataOutputStream(new FileOutputStream("my.txt"));
d.writeFloat(3.142 );
```

Table 12.4 *Methods for the DataOutputStream class.*

Method	Description
write(byte[ ])	Reads into an array of bytes.
write(byte[ ], int start , int len)	Writes into an array of bytes, the staring point and number of bytes to be written are specified.
writeBoolean( )	Writes a boolean.
writeByte( )	Writes a byte.
writeBytes( )	Writes a string as a series of bytes.
writeChar( )	Writes a 16 bit character.
writeChars( )	Writes a string as a series of characters.
writeDouble( )	Writes a 64 bit double integer.
writeFloat( )	Writes a 32 bit floating point number.
writeInt( )	Writes a 32 bit integer.
writeLong( )	Writes a 64 bit long integer.
writeShort( )	Writes a 16 bit short integer.
writeUTF( )	Writes a string in UTF format.

A list of the methods is shown in table 12.4.

The *PipedOutputStream* class

This class must be used in conjunction with the *PipedInputStream* class which provides a pipe for data transfer between threads. To set up the input stream:

PipedInputStream input = PipedInputStream( );

This stream can be picked up by a corresponding piped output stream:

PipedOutputStream output = PipedOutputStream(input);

13

Modifiers and Packages

Introduction

One important aspect of good programming, and of object oriented programming in particular, is that you can break your applet or application into self contained sections and limit the access to these sections. Modifiers allow you to do this. They are a comprehensive set of prefixes, used when defining a class, method or variable.

In this chapter you will learn:

- What access control is.
- How to use modifiers to control access to classes, methods and variables.
- What packages are and how to use them.

Access control

You can control the degree of access that one class has to another class by using one of the four access control modifiers:

- *public.*
- *private.*
- *protected.*
- *package.*

for example:

> *private class MyClass {*
>
>   ...
>
> *}*

These modifiers can also be applied to methods and variables within a class, for example:

> *public int myMethod( ) {*
> *public int myInt;*

The four access control modifiers offer varying degrees of visibility as shown in fig. 13.1.

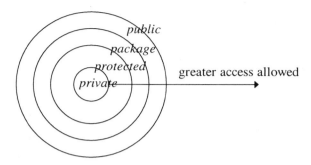

Fig. 13.1 Controlling access.

We are going to look at each of these four access control modifiers in turn.

The *public* access modifier

The *public* access modifier is used to make a class, method or variable visible and available to another class in the application or applet, for example:

```
public class MyPublicClass {
    public void myPublicMethod ( ) {
        public int myPublicInt;
        public String myPublicString;
        .....
    }
}
```

The class, methods and variables are all available throughout the application.

The *private* access modifier

The *private* access modifier is at the opposite end of the spectrum from *public*. A *private* method or variable is invisible to any class apart from the one in which it is defined, for example:

```
private class MyPrivateClass {
    private void myPrivateMethod ( ) {
        private float myPrivateFloat;
        private String myPrivateString;
        .....
    }
}
```

Ideally you should have as much *private* as possible to limit access. This tends to produce fewer bugs in applications.

The *public* and *private* access modifiers are at the opposite ends of the spectrum and there are two further levels of access control, which are useful, *package* and *protected*.

The *package* access modifier

The *package* access modifier is the default. In Java a group of related source files is collected together in a package. We have already used the packages supplied with Java such as *java.awt* in earlier chapters. If you do not specify any access control modifier then it is assumed that the package is protected. Early versions of Java do not support the package modifier explicitly - if you want this level of access control simply do not specify any access control modifier, for example:

```
public class MyPublicClass {
    void myPackageMethod ( ) {
        private float myPrivateFloat;
        String myPackageString;
        .....
    }
}
```

The *public* class *MyPublicClass* has the *myPackageMethod* which has an implicit *package* level of access control. The string also has an implicit *package* modifier.

This level of access makes the class, method or variable visible only to other classes in the same package.

The *protected* access modifier

The *protected* level offers more protection than the *package* level, but less than the *private*.

A class, method or variable which is protected is visible only to its subclasses. Two classes can be within the same package if one is not a subclass of the other, however subclasses will always share the same package as their superclass.

Accessor methods

Variables should have the maximum level of protection, ideally *private*. If you do use *public* variables they can be viewed and changed from anywhere within your applet or application. This makes the job of finding bugs even harder. There is no way, using the access control modifiers alone, that you can allow other classes to read your variable, but not to be able to write to it. This is a common problem in all object oriented systems, fortunately there is a solution to it using accessor methods.

This example looks at a *private* variable which we want to allow other classes to view, but not to change:

```
public class MyPublicClass {
    private String myPrivateString;
    ....
}
```

This defines *myPrivateString* as a *private* string. To allow any class to view the string you must add a *public* method to the class:

```
public String myPrivateStringRead {
    return myPrivateString;
}
```

Since this method is *public* it is visible to all classes. When it is called it returns the value of *myPrivateString*.

If you decide that in addition to allowing any class to view the variable you want to allow other subclasses to write to it, you add another accessor method to the *MyPublicClass* class:

```
protected void myPrivateStringWrite(String s) {
    myPrivateString = s;
}
```

Since this method is protected it only allows subclasses or *MyPublicClass* to use it. The new value of *myPrivateString* is passed as a parameter and assigned to it.

There is a contradiction in the Java documentation about giving variables and methods the same name. The formal definition of the language says that it cannot be done, but the compiler seems to cope with it.

Within *MyPublicClass* you do not need to use the accessor methods to read or write to *MyPublicClass*, but it is good programming practice to do so.

The *final* modifier

The *final* modifier, like the access control modifiers, can be applied to classes, methods and variables.

When you declare a class to be *final*, the class cannot have any subclasses:

```
public final MyFinalClass {
    ...
}
```

When a variable is declared as *final* it cannot be modified, that is, the variable becomes a constant:

```
public final MyFinalClass {
    public final String myString = "This string cannot be changed";
```

```
        ...
    }
```

A *final* variable is read in the same way as any other *public* variable (*MyFinalClass.MyString*), but it cannot be changed.

You cannot use *final* with any local variables, since these do not accept any modifiers including *final*.

Methods can also be declared as *final*. When a method is *final* it cannot be overridden by any of its subclasses. The main reason for declaring a method to be *final* is for efficiency. If the compiler is told that a method cannot be overridden by another method, it can compile your code more quickly. There are also improvements in the execution speed when *final* is used.

Using packages

We have used the packages supplied with Java extensively so far, and looked at the access modifiers which can limit access to a package, but we have not looked at how to create packages. In this section we look at the benefits of using packages and how to create them.

Why use packages?

Packages are a way of grouping classes and their subclasses into a single unit. The classes in a package should have a similar function, for example working with graphics, or input-output. When you are writing small applets the management of your classes is fairly straightforward, but as your applets increase in size and complexity, packages are helpful in managing your class structure. This becomes especially important if more than one programmer is working on an applet, since it allows each programmer or team working on different aspects of the project to develop their own packages with defined interfaces.

One problem that may arise when large applications are written by more than one person, is that there are certain common names that you might want to give to classes. For example, a group of programmers working independently on an applet might want to create a class called *Initialise* or *ErrorHandler*, which will cause conflicts. One of the key aims of Java and object oriented programming is that reusable classes will be created and made available to programmers so that the same code is not written repeatedly by different people. Sort routines which will put a list of items in alphabetical or size order must have been written literally millions of time in the past 20 years. In Java a *sort* class could be created which everyone could use, saving a great deal of time duplicating work that someone else has already done. Since there are potentially vast numbers of Java classes which may be available in the future the problem of classes being created which have the same name is a major one. Fortunately it is a problem which is completely solved by using packages.

Class names within a package have to be unique, but different packages can contain the same class names, for example two packages called *myIO* and *myGraphics* both contain a class called *Initialise* but they are distinguished as *myIO.Initialise* and *myGraphics.Initialise*.

If you want to create a class you use a *package* statement as the first entry in a source file, and then you follow it with the class definitions, for example:

> *package myPackage;*
>
> *public class MyIOClass extends MyClass {*
>   ...
> *}*

Each class within a package will have its own file, with a *class* extension.

Packages can be broken down into smaller packages, for example the *java.awt package* is broken down into *java.awt.image*, *java.awt.peer* and *java.awt.test*. This hierarchy of packages is reflected in the directory structure on your computer, with each package being in its own directory and each component of that package being in a sub-directory. This directory hierarchy for the Java packages is shown in fig. 13.2, showing the directory structure of the disk containing the Java packages.

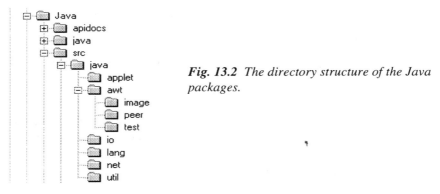

Fig. 13.2 *The directory structure of the Java packages.*

The class file for the *BufferedInputStream* class in the *java.io* package will be in the file *java/io/BufferedInputStream.class*.

If you want to create a sub package of *myPackage* called *myGraphicsPackage* you do it like this:

> *package myPackage.myGraphicsPackage;*
>
> *public class MyCircleClass extends MyGraphicsClass {*
>   ...
> *}*

The source and class files for *myPackage* must be in a directory (in Windows 95 terminology, a directory is called a folder) called *myPackage*, and the *MyGraphics* package must be below that. The class defined above must be in a file called

...*myPackage\myGraphicsClass\myCircleClass.class*, the source file must be in the same directory but will have a file extension of .java.

This is a simple but powerful system which will have benefits in the future. It is anticipated that a company which is producing its own packages will use its name as the top level directory, for example if Borland produced a graphics package it could be called *borland.graphics*. Remember that classes always start with a capital while packages do not, except for one situation. Sun Microsystems are encouraging package producers to prefix their package name with main Internet domains such as COM and EDU, so the full name for the Borland package would be *COM.borland.graphics*, the names of these Internet domains are always in capitals.

Importing packages

If you want to refer to a class in a package there are two ways in which you can do it. The first is to put the name of the package before the class name, for example *myPackage.Myclass*. This can be bit tedious if the class name is long. An easier way of doing this is to import the class:

> *import java.awt.Button;*

If you want to import many *public* classes you can use a wildcard:

> *import.java.awt.*;*

This does not import the packages below *java.awt* in the hierarchy, such as *java.awt.image*. To import this package you need to specify:

> *import.java.awt.image.*;*

When you have imported a class you do not need to prefix the classes defined within the package with the package name, for example after importing *java.awt.Button* you can create objects as shown below:

> *import java.awt.Button;*
> *Button myButton;*

You do not need to write:

> *java.awt.Button myButton;*

There is a problem with using this shorthand notation. One of the major reasons for using packages is so that class names can be reused within each package. If I decide to create a new class also called *Button* and have the following code it is unclear what is intended:

> *import java.awt.Button;*
> *import myPackage.Button;*
> *...*
> *Button myButton;*

The *Button* class is not uniquely defined and the compiler would flag an error. You could overcome the problem by explicitly stating:

> *myPackage.Button myButton;*
> *java.awt.Button yourButton;*

The *import* statements must be placed after the package definitions, but before you define any classes.

The *java.lang* package

In you look at the class hierarchies in the appendices you will see that the *java.lang* package has classes such as *boolean*, *char*, *int*, in fact all the primitive data types found in Java.

The classes of the *java.lang* package are automatically imported into your applet or application. so that you can write:

> *int myInteger;*

You do not need to specify the package explicitly by:

> *java.lang.int myInteger;*

14
Java and C++

Introduction

When a C++ programmer first see Java, the immediate reaction is that Java is really the same as C++. While the two languages have much in common there are some significant differences between them that can cause problems if you are not aware of them.

In this chapter you will learn about the differences between Java and C++ including:

- The supported data types.
- The use of command line arguments.
- Using strings.
- Exception handling.

We look at each of these areas in turn.

Data types

Java does not support pointers. This will be a shock to C++ programmers, but since Java is designed to work on any host computer with the browser environment, a Java applet cannot reference the memory of a computer whose organisation and memory it does know about. However, Java does pass values objects and arrays by reference (that is specifying the address of the object) rather than by value.

Java does not support *struct* or *union*, instead composite data types are achieved by using class definitions.

Java does not support unsigned data types.

The boolean data type is not an integer as it is in C++, it can be assigned only two values either *true* or *false*.

159

Using strings

Strings in C++ are null terminated strings, that is that have a '\0' character at the end. In Java strings are objects and are not terminated by a null. One of the most common errors in C++ programs is an out of bounds array reference, that is defining an array as having *n* elements and trying to address an element greater than *n*. This can lead to unpredictable results. Java rigorously ensures that both array and string bounds are not exceeded. The *String* class in Java allows strings to be assigned to each other rather than being copied character by character as happens in C++.

Command line arguments

In C++ when you run a program, two parameters are passed to the application:

- *argc*, the number of arguments on the command line.
- *argv*, a pointer to an array of strings containing the arguments.

In Java programs there is only one parameter passed to the application:
- *args*, an array of strings containing the arguments.

The number of arguments can be found from using the *length( )* method of the array.
In C++ programs the whole of the command line is passed to the program, for example if you ran an application called *sort* and specified an input file to be sorted and an output file to hold the result the command line would be:

   sort infile outfile

The first argument would be *sort*, the second and third *infile* and *outfile*.
The corresponding command line for a Java application would be:

   javac sort infile outfile

The first argument is *infile*.
In Java applets parameters are passed via the HTML file using the PARAM NAME and VALUE attributes.

Exception handling

When an exception occurs, Java provides a way of cleaning up the method before leaving the code which handles the exception. This is done in Java by enclosing the code within a *finally* block. The code within the *finally* block is always executed no matter what happens within the *try* block. This is covered in detail in chapter 8.
There is no equivalent to the *finally* block in C++.

Miscellaneous differences

- Java does not support *goto*, although it is a reserved word.
- C++ allows you to pass a variable number of arguments to a program, this is not allowed in Java.
- The + operator can be used to concatenate strings.
- The >>> operator performs an unsigned logical right shift.
- Java does not support the *const* keyword.
- Java does not support functions. Methods are used instead of functions.
- In Java memory management is automatic. There is no equivalent to the *malloc* function.

Appendix A

Java Packages

Introduction

This appendix gives some details of Java that you may need to know, such as a complete list of reserved words and characters, and details of all the classes in the Java packages.

Reserved words

Reserved words in Java have a special meaning and cannot be used for any other purpose.

Table A.1 Reserved words.

abstract	continue	future	long	rest	transient
boolean	default	generic	native	return	try
break	do	goto	new	short	var
byte	double	if	null	static	void
case	else	implements	operator	sure	volatile
cast	extends	imports	outer	switch	while
catch	final	inner	package	synchronized	
char	finally	instanceof	private	this	
class	float	int	protected	throw	
const	for	interface	public	throws	

Reserved characters

The characters listed in table A.2 cannot be used in a variable name, since they have special meanings in Java.

Table A.2 *Reserved characters.*

+	-	!	%	^	&	*	|	-	/	>	<
(	)	{	}	[	]	;	?	:	,	.	=

Java operators

This is a complete list of all the operators in Java.

Table A.3 *The Java operators.*

Operator	Meaning	Operator	Meaning
+	Addition.	<<	Left Shift.
-	Subtraction.	>>	Right Shift.
*	Multiplication.	>>>	Zero fill right shift.
/	Division.	-	Complement.
%	Modulus.	=	Assignment.
<	Less than.	++	Increment.
>	Greater than.	--	Decrement.
>=	Greater than or equal to.	+=	Add and assign.
<=	Less than or equal to.	-=	Minus and assign.
==	Equal.	*=	Multiply and assign.
!=	Not equal.	/=	Divide and assign.
&&	Logical AND.	%=	Modulus and assign.
||	Logical OR.	&=	AND and assign.
!	Logical NOT.	|=	OR and assign.
&	AND.	<<=	Left shift and assign.
|	OR.	>>=	Right shift and assign.
^	XOR.	>>>=	Zero fill, right shift and assign.

Java data types

Integer:

- *byte* 8 bits.
- *short* 16 bits.
- *int* 32 bits.
- *long* 64 bits.

Floating point:

- *float* 32 bits.
- *double* 64 bits.

Character:

- *char* 16 bit unsigned integer assigned the Unicode character number.

Boolean:

- boolean true or false.

The Java class library

This section lists the classes and exceptions in the Java class library which is divided into packages.

The *java.awt* package

This is a complete list of the classes in the *java.awt* package.

Table A.4 The java.awt package.

Class	Description
BorderLayout	A layout manager for organising components.
Button	A labelled button component.
Canvas	A *Canvas* component for drawing.
CardLayout	A layout manager for a container that contains several 'cards'. Only one card is visible at a time, allowing you to flip through the cards.
Checkbox	A *Checkbox* component, that has either a true of false state.
CheckboxGroup	A group of checkboxes. Only one checkbox, at most, in the group may be set to true, the rest are false.
CheckboxMenuItem	This class produces a checkbox that represents a choice in a menu.
Choice	A pop-up menu of choices. The current choice is displayed as the title of the menu.
Color	A class to encapsulate RGB Colours.
Component	A generic Abstract Window Toolkit component.
Container	A component that can contain other AWT components.
Dialog	A window that takes input from the user. The default layout for a dialog is *BorderLayout*
Dimension	A class to encapsulate a width and a height.
Event	*Event* is a platform-independent class that represents events from the user or the system.
FileDialog	The *FileDialog* class displays a file selection dialog and allows the user to make a selection.
FlowLayout	A layout manager that arranges buttons left to right in a panel.

Font	A class that produces a representations of fonts.
FontMetrics	A class for holding information font metrics.
Frame	A top-level window with a title.
Graphics	*Graphics* is the abstract base class for producing shapes and objects.
GridBagConstraints	*GridBagConstraints* specifies constraints for components set out using the *GridBagLayout* class.
GridBagLayout	*GridBagLayout* is a flexible layout organiser that aligns components vertically and horizontally, without requiring that the components be the same size. Each component is described by a *GridBagConstraints* instance.
GridLayout	A layout manager for a container that sets out grids.
Image	The image class is an abstract representation of a bit map.
Insets	The distance of the container from the inside edges of the window.
Label	A component that displays a single line of read-only text.
List	A scrolling list of text items.
MediaTracker	A utility class to track the status of a number of media objects, such as video and audio.
Menu	A *Menu* contains menu items and is a component of a menu bar.
MenuBar	A menu container.
MenuComponent	The super class of all menu related components.
MenuItem	A single item in a menu.
Panel	A *Panel* is a generic container component.
Point	x, y co-ordinates.
Polygon	A list of x and y co-ordinates.
Rectangle	A *Rectangle* defined by the x, y of the top left corner, the width and the height.
Scrollbar	A *Scrollbar* component.
TextArea	A scrollable multi-line area for displaying or editing text.
TextComponent	A *TextComponent* is a superclass of all component that allows the editing of some text.
TextField	A *TextField* component allows the editing of only one line of text.
Toolkit	It is used for binding the abstract AWT classes to a particular implementation.
Window	A top-level window with no borders and no menu bar. It is the superclass of the *Frame* and *Dialog* classes.

Exception index for *java.awt*

Table A.5 *Exception index for java.awt.*

Exception	Description
AWTException	Indicates that an AWT exception has occurred.

The *java.awt.image* package

This is a complete list of the classes in the *java.awt.image* package.

Table A.6 *The java.awt package.*

Class	Description
ColorModel	A class that encapsulates the methods for translating from pixel values to alpha and RGB colour components for an image.
CropImageFilter	A filter class which is used for cropping images. This class extends the *ImageFilter* Class to extract a rectangular region of an image.
DirectColorModel	A *ColorModel* class that manages a translation from pixel values to alpha and RGB colour components for pixels.
FilteredImageSource	An implementation of the *ImageProducer* interface which takes an existing image and a filter object and produces a filtered version of the original image.
ImageFilter	This class implements a filter that takes data from an *ImageProducer*, modifies it and passes it to an *ImageConsumer*.
IndexColorModel	This class specifies a translation from pixel values to alpha, red, green, and blue colour components for pixels which represent indices into a fixed colour map.
MemoryImageSource	This class is an implementation of the *ImageProducer* interface which uses an array to build up an image.
PixelGrabber	The *PixelGrabber* class implements an *ImageConsumer* which can be attached to an *Image* or *ImageProducer* object to retrieve a subset of the pixels in that image.
RGBFiterImage	An abstract class for creating an ImageFilter which modifies the pixels of an RGB image.

Exception index for *java.awt.image*

There are no exceptions for this class.

The *java.awt.peer* package

This is a complete list of the interfaces in the *java.awt.peer* package.

Every member of this package has a corresponding class in the *java.awt.* package. The names are different in that *peer* is added to the class name. These interfaces provide a platform independent implementation of the platform specific *java.awt* classes.

Since the behaviour of these classes is very similar to the class from which they inherit, they are listed below, but not described.

Table A.7 *The java.awt.peer package.*

Class Index	Class index	Class Index
ButtonPeer	*DialogPeer*	*MenuItemPeer*
CanvasPeer	*FileDialogPeer*	*MenuPeer*
CheckboxMenuItemPeer	*FramePeer*	*PanelPeer*
CheckboxPeer	*LabelPer*	*ScrollbarPeer*
ChoicePeer	*ListPeer*	*TextAreaPeer*
ComponentPeer	*MenuBarPeer*	*TextComponentPeer*
ContainerPeer	*MenuComponentPeer*	*TextFieldPeer*
		WindowPeer

Exception index for *java.awt.peer*

There are no exceptions for this class.

The *java.io* package

This is a complete list of the classes in the *java.io* package.

Table A.8 *The java.io package.*

Class Index	Description
BufferedInputStream	This stream allows you read in characters from a stream without causing a read to a device such as a disk every time. The data is read into a buffer, so that subsequent reads are carried out faster, as the buffer rather than the disk has to be referenced.
BufferedOutputStream	This is the converse of the *BufferedInputStream*. This stream allows you to write characters to a stream without causing a write to a physical device every time. The data is first written into a buffer. Data is written to the actual stream either when the buffer is full, or when the stream is flushed.

ByteArrayInputStream	This class implements an input stream from a byte array.
ByteArrayOutputStream	This class implements a buffer that can be used as an output stream. The buffer grows when data is written to the stream.
DataInputStream	An input stream that lets you read primitive Java data types such as integers from a stream.
DataOutputStream	This class lets you write primitive Java data types to a stream.
File	This class represents a file name of the host file system. If a file name or path is used it is assumed that the host's file name conventions are used.
FileInputStream	An input stream from a file constructed from a file descriptor or a file name.
FileOutputStream	*FileOutputStream*, can be constructed from a file descriptor or a file name.
FilterInputStream	An abstract class representing a filtered input stream of bytes.
FilterOutputStream	An abstract class representing a filtered output stream of bytes.
InputStream	An abstract class representing an input stream of bytes. All input streams are based on this class.
LineNumberInputStream	An input stream that keeps track of line numbers.
OutputStream	Abstract class representing an output stream of bytes. All output streams are based on this class.
PipedInputStream	A thread reading from a *PipedInputStream* receives data from a thread writing to the *PipedOutputStream* it is connected to.
PipedOutputStream	The partner of *PipedInputStream*.
PrintStream	This class implements an output stream that has additional methods for printing, such as flushing every time a new line character is written. The top 8 bits of 16 bit characters are ignored.
PushbackInputStream	An input stream that has a 1 byte push back buffer.
RandomAccessFile	Random access files can be constructed from file descriptors, file names, or file objects. This class has methods which allow specified modes of access of read-only or read-write to files.
SequenceInputStream	Converts a sequence of input streams into an input stream.

| *StreamTokenizer* | A class to turn an input stream into a stream of tokens. |
| *StringBufferInputStream* | An input stream, from a *String* buffer. |

Exception index for *java.io*

Table A.9 Exception index for java.io.

Exception	Description
EOFException	Signals that and EOF has been reached unexpectedly during input.
FileNotFoundException	Signals that a file was not found.
IOException	Signals that an I/O exception has occurred.
InterruptedIOException	Signals that an I/O operation has been interrupted.
UTFDataFormatException	Signals that a malformed UTF-8 string has been read in a data input stream.

The *java.lang* package

This is a complete list of the classes in the *java.lang* package.

Table A.10 The java.lang package.

Class Index	Description
Boolean	The *Boolean* class provides an object wrapper for *Boolean* data values. Since booleans are not objects in Java, they need to be wrapped in a boolean instance.
Character	The *Character* class provides an object wrapper for character data values.
Class	Class objects contain runtime representations of classes. Every object in the system is an instance of some class.
ClassLoader	*ClassLoader* is an abstract class that can be used to define a policy for loading Java classes into the runtime environment.
Double	The *Double* class provides an object wrapper for double length data values.
Float	The *Float* class provides an object wrapper for floating point data values.
Integer	The *Integer* class is a wrapper for integer values.
Long	The *Long* class provides an object wrapper for long data values.
Math	The standard Math library for the methods in this class.
Number	*Number* is an abstract superclass for number classes: *Integer*, *Long*, *Float* and *Double*.

Object	The root of the class hierarchy. Every class in the system has *Object* as its parent.
Process	This class provides abstract behaviour for spawned processes.
Runtime	This class allows access to the Java run time.
SecurityManager	An abstract class that can be subclassed to implement a security policy.
String	A general class of objects to represent character strings.
StringBuffer	This class is a buffer for characters that can automatically grow on demand.
System	This class provides a system-independent interface to system functionality such as the standard input and output streams.
Thread	This class provides a way of managing threads.
ThreadGroup	A group of threads and thread groups.
Throwable	An object of this class indicates that an exceptional condition has occurred.

Exception index for *java.lang*

Table A.11 Exception index for java.lang.

Exception	Description
ArithmeticException	Indicates that an exceptional arithmetic condition has occurred, for example, dividing by zero.
ArrayIndexOutOfBoundsException	Indicates that an invalid array index has been used.
ArrayStoreException	An attempt has been made to store the wrong type of object to an array.
ClassCastException	Indicates that an invalid cast has occurred.
ClassNotFoundException	Indicates that a class could not be found.
CloneNotSupportedException	Indicates that an attempt has been made to clone an object that does not want to be cloned.
Exception	Exception are a form of throwable objects that normal programs may wish to try and catch.
IllegalAccessException	Indicates that a particular method could not be found.
IllegalArgumentException	Indicates that an illegal argument exception has occurred.

IllegalMonitorStateException	Indicates that a monitor operation has been attempted when the monitor is in an invalid state.
IllegalThreadStateException	An exception indicating that a thread is not in a legal state for the requested operation.
IndexOutOfBoundsException	Indicates that an index of some sort is out of bounds.
InstantiationException	Indicates that an attempt has been made to instantiate an abstract class or an interface and has failed.
InterruptedException	An exception indicated that some thread has interrupted this thread.
NegativeArraySizeException	Indicates that an attempt has been made to create an array with negative size.
NoSuchMethodException	Indicates that a particular method could not be found.
NullPointerException	Indicates the illegal use of a null pointer.
NumberFormatException	Indicates that an invalid number format has occurred.
RuntimeException	An exception that can reasonably occur during the execution of a Java program by the Virtual machine.
SecurityException	Indicates that a security exception has occurred.
StringIndexOutOfBoundsException	Signals that a string index is out of range.

The *java.util* package

This is a complete list of the classes in the *java.util* package.

Table A.12 *The java.util package.*

Class Index	Description
BitSet	A set of bits. The set automatically grows as required.
Date	A wrapper for a date.
Dictionary	An abstract class which maps keys to values.
Hashtable	Hashtable class. Maps keys to values.
Observable	This class should be subclassed by observable objects.
Properties	This class is basically a hashtable for reading and changing persistent properties of a system or class.
Random	A *Random* class generates a stream of random numbers.
Stack	A Last-In-First-Out(LIFO) stack of objects.
StringTokenizer	Controls simple linear tokenization of a string.
Vector	An array of objects.

Exception index for *java.util*

Table A.13 *Exception index for java.util.*

Exception	Description
EmptyStackException	Indicates that the stack is empty.
NoSuchElementException	Indicates that a specified element does not exist.

The *java.net* package

This is a complete list of the classes in the *java.net* package.

Table A.14 *The java.net package.*

Class Index	Description
ContentHandler	A class to read data from a URLConnection and construct an Object.
DatagramPacket	A class that represents a datagram packet containing packet data, packet length, Internet addresses and port.
DatagramSocket	The datagram socket class implements unreliable datagrams.
InetAddress	A class that represents Internet addresses.
ServerSocket	The server Socket class.
Socket	The client Socket class.
SocketImpl	This is the Socket implementation class. It is an abstract class that must be subclassed to provide an actual implementation.
URL	The URL represents a Uniform Reference Locator, a reference to an object on the World Wide Web. This is a constant object, once it is created, its fields cannot be changed.
URLConnection	A class to represent an active connection to an object represented by a URL. It is an abstract class that must be subclassed to implement a connection.
URLEncoder	Turns strings of text into URL encoded format.
URLStreamHandler	Abstract class for URL stream openers. Subclasses of this class know how to create streams for particular protocol types.

Exception index for *java.net*

Table A.15 *Exception index for java.net.*

Exception	Description
MalformedURLException	Signals that a malformed URL has occurred.
ProtocolException	Signals when connect gets an EPROTO. This exception is specifically caught in the class *Socket*.
SocketException	Signals that an error occurred while attempting to use a socket.
UnknownHostException	Signals that the address of the server specified by a network client could not be resolved.
UnknownServiceException	Signals that an unknown service exception has occurred.

The *java.applet* package

There is only one class in the java.applet package package.

Table A.16 *The java.applet package.*

Class Index	Description
Applet	The base applet class

Exception index for *java.applet*

There are no exceptions for this class.

Appendix B

Class Hierarchies

Introduction

This appendix gives an alphabetical listing of the Java classes and interfaces.

Class hierarchy

class java.lang.Object

    interface java.applet.*AppletContext*

    interface java.applet.*AppletStub*

    interface java.applet.*AudioClip*

    class java.util.*BitSet* (implements java.lang.Cloneable)

    class java.lang.*Boolean*

    class java.awt.*BorderLayout* (implements java.awt.LayoutManager)

    interface java.awt.peer.*ButtonPeer* (extends java.awt.peer.ComponentPeer)

    interface java.awt.peer.*CanvasPeer* (extends java.awt.peer.ComponentPeer)

    class java.awt.*CardLayout* (implements java.awt.LayoutManager)

    class java.lang.*Character*

    class java.awt.*CheckboxGroup*

    interface java.awt.peer.*CheckboxMenuItemPeer* (extends java.awt.peer.MenuItemPeer)

    interface java.awt.peer.*CheckboxPeer* (extends java.awt.peer.ComponentPeer)

    interface java.awt.peer.*ChoicePeer* (extends java.awt.peer.ComponentPeer)

    class java.lang.*Class*

```
├─ class java.lang.ClassLoader
├─ interface java.lang.Cloneable
├─ class java.awt.Color
├─ class java.awt.image.ColorModel
│       ├─ class java.awt.image.DirectColorModel
│       └─ class java.awt.image.IndexColorModel
├─ class java.lang.Compiler
├─ class java.awt.Component (implements java.awt.image.ImageObserver)
│       ├─ class java.awt.Button
│       ├─ class java.awt.Canvas
│       ├─ class java.awt.Checkbox
│       ├─ class java.awt.Choice
│       ├─ class java.awt.Container
│       │       ├─ class java.awt.Panel
│       │       │       └─ class java.applet.Applet
│       │       └─ class java.awt.Window
│       │               ├─ class java.awt.Dialog
│       │               │       └─ class java.awt.FileDialog
│       │               └─ class java.awt.Frame (implements java.awt.MenuContainer)
│       ├─ class java.awt.Label
│       ├─ class java.awt.List
│       ├─ class java.awt.Scrollbar
│       └─ class java.awt.TextComponent
│               ├─ class java.awt.TextArea
│               └─ class java.awt.TextField
├─ interface java.awt.peer.ComponentPeer
├─ Interface sun.tools.java.Constants (extends sun.tools.java.RuntimeConstants)
└─ interface java.awt.peer.ContainerPeer (extends java.awt.peer.ComponentPeer)
```

class java.net.*ContentHandler*

interface java.net.*ContentHandlerFactory*

interface java.io.*DataInput*

interface java.io.*DataOutput*

class java.net.*DatagramPacket*

class java.net.*DatagramSocket*

class java.util.*Date*

interface sun.tools.debug.*DebuggerCallback*

interface java.awt.peer.*DialogPeer* (extends java.awt.peer.WindowPeer)

class java.util.*Dictionary*

       class java.util.*Hashtable* (implements java.lang.Cloneable)

            class java.util.*Properties*

class java.awt.*Dimension*

interface java.util.*Enumeration*

class java.awt.*Event*

class sun.tools.debug.*Field*

       class sun.tools.debug.*RemoteField* (implements sun.tools.debug.AgentConstants)

class java.io.*File*

class java.io.*FileDescriptor*

interface java.awt.peer.*FileDialogPeer* (extends java.awt.peer.DialogPeer)

interface java.io.*FilenameFilter*

class java.awt.image.*FilteredImageSource* (implements java.awt.image.ImageProducer)

class java.awt.*FlowLayout* (implements java.awt.LayoutManager)

class java.awt.*Font*

class java.awt.*FontMetrics*

interface java.awt.peer.*FramePeer* (extends java.awt.peer.WindowPeer)

class java.awt.*Graphics*

class java.awt.*GridBagConstraints* (implements java.lang.Cloneable) class java.awt.*GridBagLayout* (implements java.awt.LayoutManager)

class java.awt.*GridLayout* (implements java.awt.LayoutManager)

class java.awt.*Image*

interface java.awt.image.*ImageConsumer*

class java.awt.image.*ImageFilter* (implements java.awt.image.ImageConsumer, java.lang.Cloneable)

> class java.awt.image.*CropImageFilter*
>
> class java.awt.image.*RGBImageFilter*

interface java.awt.image.*ImageObserver*

interface java.awt.image.*ImageProducer*

class java.net.*InetAddress*

class java.io.*InputStream*

> class java.io.*ByteArrayInputStream*
>
> class java.io.*FileInputStream*
>
> class java.io.*FilterInputStream*
>
> > class java.io.*BufferedInputStream*
> >
> > class java.io.*DataInputStream* (implements java.io.DataInput)
> >
> > class java.io.*LineNumberInputStream*
> >
> > class java.io.*PushbackInputStream*
>
> class java.io.*PipedInputStream*
>
> class java.io.*SequenceInputStream*
>
> class java.io.*StringBufferInputStream*

class java.awt.*Insets* (implements java.lang.Cloneable)

interface java.awt.peer.*LabelPeer* (extends java.awt.peer.ComponentPeer)

interface java.awt.*LayoutManager*

interface java.awt.peer.*ListPeer* (extends java.awt.peer.ComponentPeer)

class sun.tools.debug.*LocalVariable*

> class sun.tools.debug.*RemoteStackVariable*

class java.lang.*Math*

class java.awt.*MediaTracker*

class java.awt.image.*MemoryImageSource*
(implements java.awt.image.ImageProducer)

interface java.awt.peer.*MenuBarPeer* (extends
java.awt.peer.MenuComponentPeer)

class java.awt.*MenuComponent*

    class java.awt.*MenuBar* (implements java.awt.MenuContainer)

    class java.awt.*MenuItem*

        class java.awt.*CheckboxMenuItem*

        class java.awt.*Menu* (implements java.awt.MenuContainer)

interface java.awt.peer.*MenuComponentPeer*

interface java.awt.*MenuContainer*

interface java.awt.peer.*MenuItemPeer* (extends java.awt.peer.MenuComponentPeer)

interface java.awt.peer.*MenuPeer* (extends java.awt.peer.MenuItemPeer)

class java.lang.*Number*

    class java.lang.*Double*

    class java.lang.*Float*

    class java.lang.*Integer*

    class java.lang.*Long*

class java.util.*Observable*

interface java.util.*Observer*

class java.io.*OutputStream*

    class java.io.*ByteArrayOutputStream*

    class java.io.*FileOutputStream*

    class java.io.*FilterOutputStream*

        class java.io.*BufferedOutputStream*

        class java.io.*DataOutputStream* (implements java.io.DataOutput)

        class java.io.*PrintStream*

    class java.io.*PipedOutputStream*

interface java.awt.peer.*PanelPeer* (extends java.awt.peer.ContainerPeer) class java.awt.image.*PixelGrabber* (implements java.awt.image.ImageConsumer)

class java.awt.*Point*

class java.awt.*Polygon*

class java.lang.*Process*

class java.util.*Random*

class java.io.*RandomAccessFile* (implements
java.io.DataOutput, java.io.DataInput)

class java.awt.*Rectangle*

class sun.tools.debug.*RemoteDebugger*

class sun.tools.debug.*RemoteValue*
(implements sun.tools.debug.AgentConstants)

    class sun.tools.debug.*RemoteBoolean*

    class sun.tools.debug.*RemoteByte*

    class sun.tools.debug.*RemoteChar*

    class sun.tools.debug.*RemoteDouble*

    class sun.tools.debug.*RemoteFloat*

    class sun.tools.debug.*RemoteInt*

    class sun.tools.debug.*RemoteLong*

    class sun.tools.debug.*RemoteObject*

        class sun.tools.debug.*RemoteArray*

        class sun.tools.debug.*RemoteClass*

        class sun.tools.debug.*RemoteString*

        class sun.tools.debug.*RemoteThread*

        class sun.tools.debug.*RemoteThreadGroup*

    class sun.tools.debug.*RemoteShort*

interface java.lang.*Runnable*

class java.lang.*Runtime*

interface sun.tools.java.*RuntimeConstants*

interface java.awt.peer.*ScrollbarPeer* (extends java.awt.peer.ComponentPeer)

class java.lang.*SecurityManager*

class java.net.*ServerSocket*

class java.net.*Socket*

class java.net.*SocketImpl*

interface java.net.*SocketImplFactory*

class sun.tools.debug.*StackFrame*

  class sun.tools.debug.*RemoteStackFrame*

class java.io.*StreamTokenizer*

class java.lang.*String*

class java.lang.*StringBuffer*

class java.util.*StringTokenizer* (implements java.util.Enumeration)

class java.lang.*System*

interface java.awt.peer.*TextAreaPeer* (extends java.awt.peer.TextComponentPeer)

interface java.awt.peer.*TextComponentPeer* (extends java.awt.peer.ComponentPeer)

interface java.awt.peer.*TextFieldPeer* (extends java.awt.peer.TextComponentPeer)

class java.lang.*Thread* (implements java.lang.Runnable)

class java.lang.*ThreadGroup*

class java.lang.*Throwable*

  class java.lang.*Error*

    class java.awt.*AWTError*

    class java.lang.*LinkageError*

      class java.lang.*ClassCircularityError*

      class java.lang.*ClassFormatError*

      class java.lang.*IncompatibleClassChangeError*

        class java.lang.*AbstractMethodError*

        class java.lang.*IllegalAccessError*

        class java.lang.*InstantiationError*

        class java.lang.*NoSuchFieldError*

        class java.lang.*NoSuchMethodError*

class java.lang.*NoClassDefFoundError*

class java.lang.*UnsatisfiedLinkError*

class java.lang.*VerifyError*

class java.lang.*ThreadDeath*

class java.lang.*VirtualMachineError*

class java.lang.*InternalError*

class java.lang.*OutOfMemoryError*

class java.lang.*StackOverflowError*

class java.lang.*UnknownError*

class java.lang.*Exception*

class java.awt.*AWTException*

class java.lang.*ClassNotFoundException*

class java.lang.*CloneNotSupportedException*

class java.io.*IOException*

class java.io.*EOFException*

class java.io.*FileNotFoundException*

class java.io.*InterruptedIOException*

class java.net.*MalformedURLException*

class java.net.*ProtocolException*

class java.net.*SocketException*

class java.io.*UTFDataFormatException*

class java.net.*UnknownHostException*

class java.net.*UnknownServiceException*

class java.lang.*IllegalAccessException*

class java.lang.*InstantiationException*

class java.lang.*InterruptedException*

class java.lang.*NoSuchMethodException*

class java.lang.*RuntimeException*

class java.lang.*ArithmeticException*

class java.lang.*ArrayStoreException*

```
class java.lang.ClassCastException
class java.util.EmptyStackException
class java.lang.IllegalArgumentException
    class java.lang.IllegalThreadStateException
    class java.lang.NumberFormatException
class java.lang.IllegalMonitorStateException
class java.lang.IndexOutOfBoundsException
    class java.lang.ArrayIndexOutOfBoundsException
    class java.lang.StringIndexOutOfBoundsException
class java.lang.NegativeArraySizeException
class java.util.NoSuchElementException
class java.lang.NullPointerException
class java.lang.SecurityException
class java.awt.Toolkit
class java.net.URL
class java.net.URLConnection
class java.net.URLEncoder
class java.net.URLStreamHandler
interface java.net.URLStreamHandlerFactory
class java.util.Vector (implements java.lang.Cloneable)
    class java.util.Stack
interface java.awt.peer.WindowPeer (extends java.awt.peer.ContainerPeer)
```

Index